# WALKING IN THE SOUTHERN UPLANDS

# About the Author

Ronald Turnbull was born in St Andrews, Scotland, into an energetic fell-walking family. In 1995 he won the Fell Running Association's long-distance trophy for a non-stop run over all the 2000ft hills of southern Scotland; his other proud achievements include the ascent of the north ridge of the Weisshorn, and finishing the Ben Nevis race in less than 2hrs. He still likes to mix some fast and challenging outings among gentler walks.

He enjoys multi-day treks, through the Highlands in particular, and has made 21 different coast-to-coast crossings of the UK. He has also slept out on over 70 UK summits. Outside the UK he likes hot, rocky areas of Europe, ideally with beaches and cheap flights. Recently he completed California's 220-mile John Muir Trail and East Lothian's 45 mile John Muir Way in a single season, and believes he is the first to have achieved this slightly perverse double. He has also started trying to understand the geology of what he's been walking and climbing on for so long.

Ronald lives in the Lowther Hills of Dumfriesshire, and most of his walking, and writing, takes place in the nearby Lake District and in the Scottish Highlands. He has seven times won Outdoor Writers and Photographers Guild Awards for Excellence for his guidebooks, outdoor books (including *The Book of the Bivvy*) and magazine articles. He has a regular column in *Lakeland Walker* and also writes in *Trail*, *Cumbria* and *The Great Outdoors*. His current, hopelessly ambitious, project is to avoid completing the Munros for at least another 20 years. Find out more at www.ronaldturnbull.co.uk.

## Other Cicerone guides by the author

*Ben Nevis and Glen Coe*
*Not the West Highland Way*
*The Book of the Bivvy*
*Three Peaks, Ten Tors*
*Walking Highland Perthshire*

*Walking in the Cairngorms*
*Walking Loch Lomond and the*
   *Trossachs*
*Walking the Lowther Hills*

# WALKING IN THE SOUTHERN UPLANDS

by Ronald Turnbull

CICERONE

2 POLICE SQUARE, MILNTHORPE, CUMBRIA LA7 7PY
www.cicerone.co.uk

© Ronald Turnbull 2015
First edition 2015
ISBN: 978 1 85284 740 1

Printed by KHL Printing, Singapore
A catalogue record for this book is available from the British Library.
All photographs are by the author.

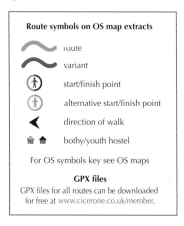

**Route symbols on OS map extracts**

| | |
|---|---|
| ～ | route |
| ～ | variant |
| (↑) | start/finish point |
| (↑) | alternative start/finish point |
| ◀ | direction of walk |
| 🏠 🏠 | bothy/youth hostel |

For OS symbols key see OS maps

**GPX files**

GPX files for all routes can be downloaded
for free at www.cicerone.co.uk/member.

## Updates to this Guide

While every effort is made by our authors to ensure the accuracy of guidebooks as they go to print, changes can occur during the lifetime of an edition. If we know of any, there will be an Updates tab on this book's page on the Cicerone website (www.cicerone.co.uk), so please check before planning your trip. We also advise that you check information about such things as transport, accommodation and shops locally. Even rights of way can be altered over time. We are always grateful for information about any discrepancies between a guidebook and the facts on the ground, sent by email to info@cicerone.co.uk or by post to Cicerone, 2 Police Square, Milnthorpe LA7 7PY, United Kingdom.

*Front cover:* Descending Merrick's Redstone Ridge towards Loch Enoch on Walk 5

# CONTENTS

*South ridge of Carlin's Cairn looking towards Corserine (Walk 7)*

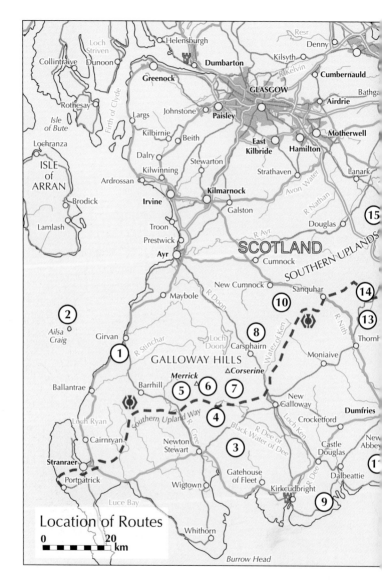

# Location of Routes

```
0            20
▮▮▮▮▮▮▮▮▮▮▮▮ km
```

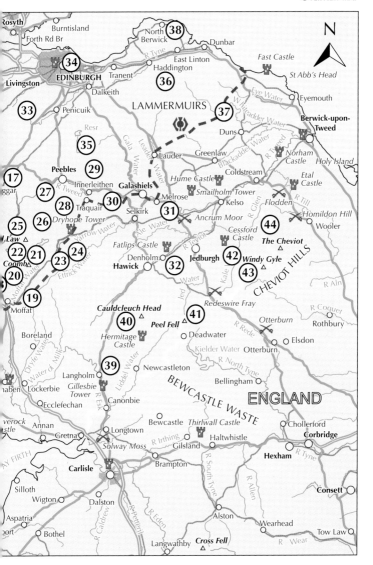

*Queensberry from Capel Water (Walk 12) – its grassy slopes are typical of the central Southern Uplands*

# INTRODUCTION

*Dun Rig and Hundleshope Heights from Kailzie Hill (Walk 28)*

From the Atlantic Ocean to the North Sea, one big line of hills stretches all the way along the southern edge of Scotland. The Southern Uplands – it's the range that's about as big as the Pennines but you've probably never been to. Here are over 80 hills of 2000ft (600m) or more – and the smaller ones are also important. And it's a country with its own character – green and gentle, but with hidden surprises.

The Lake District, Snowdonia and the Scottish Highlands – UK walkers, quite rightly, clamber their rocky ridges and queue at their summit cairns. For this writer at least, and without wanting to be impolite to the Pennines, the Southern Uplands are the UK's fourth great range. In terms of land area, it's Lakeland three times over, or six Snowdonias.

Any walking lifetime should include some time – 44 days, say – in these distinctive hills. 'Smooth classics' we can call them, where the wind sings in the grasses, and clouds drift across an empty glen with its twisting river. Here are snowfields where the only footprints belong to a fox who's just as chilly and bewildered as you are. From the huge views of the Cheviots to the mysteries of iced-over Loch Enoch, this lost bit of Scotland is your local Siberia.

## BOUNDARIES OF THE BORDERS

Logically – and indeed geologically – the Southern Uplands have their northern edge at the faultline scarp of the Southern Upland Fault, a clearly defined hill edge from Dunbar to Ballantrae. And their southern boundary is the wide vale of the Tweed. The

*The Pennine Way approaches Auchope Hut on the Border Ridge to The Cheviot (Walk 44)*

Southern Upland Way, Scotland's longest long-distance path, follows this band of high ground. Starting at the Solway, the component ranges are the granite slabs of Galloway (Section 1), Dumfriesshire's Lowthers and Carsphairn group (Section 2), the Moffat and Manor Hills (Sections 3 and 4 respectively), the Moorfoots south of Edinburgh (Sections 4 and 5), and across to the Lammermuirs above North Sea (Section 5). This main range makes up the greater part of this book.

Across on the south side of the Tweed valley, the Cheviots of the Anglo-Scottish border are linked with the main Southern Uplands by a common harsh history of the Border cattle-thieving times. And that history reflects a common geography of sheltered, fertile glens, self contained below wide miles of empty hill – ideal for cattle-raiders' ponies. This border range makes up the book's Section 6.

In between the two, the Tweed itself has a couple of quite different summits. The small volcanic lumps of Eildon and Rubers Law (both Section 4) have their own special atmosphere, steep and stony above the wide valley with its great river. And the so-called

Scottish Lowlands, north of that fault-line scarp, have similar wee treats – Tinto (Section 3) and North Berwick Law and the pokey-up Pentlands at the very edge of Edinburgh (all in Section 5). These add-on hills are pleasing in themselves, and even more so as a contrast with the big, but gently grassy, main range. Without such volcanic oddities as Arthur's Seat (at the end of Edinburgh's Royal Mile) or Ailsa Craig (several miles out to sea in the Firth of Clyde), the Southern Uplands would retain their massive grandeur but lose something of the fun.

And so this book extends itself south as far as the England–Scotland border, and runs north to Edinburgh and Glasgow. The Cheviots are approached from their Scottish side, including The Cheviot itself, which is a hill in England. ('Pending reconquest', as a Scottish Nationalist might say.)

## REAL REMOTENESS

The Southern Uplands have more real remoteness than anywhere south of the Highland Line. From Nithsdale or Eskdale or Ettrick, walkers can venture into the hills for 20km or more before the next lonely glen with its little white farmhouses and silver river. Some hills around the edges have paths formed by previous visitors, and the Pentlands are positively convivial. But in the Southern Upland heartlands, those 20km could be covered without meeting anybody else at all.

Old paths or modern grouse-shooters' tracks lead up to the airy tops. Here walkers can cover an awful lot of ground up among the cloudberry and under the open sky and the skylarks. The going is fast and grassy, across a couple, or six, or a dozen of the rounded hills.

Gaze down into hidden hollows such as Hen Hole or the Beef Tub, where cattle thieves and Covenanters lurked; walk steep-sided river valleys with grim castles; and come upon sudden views south into England or north to the Highlands along the horizon. And then descend by another old path, or by one of the stream-carved cleuchs or linns, to the Grey Mare's Tail waterfalls, or a pretty village in red sandstone, or the banks of the wide, wandering River Tweed.

In winter, the snowfields stretch, hump beyond hump, to the misty blue of Edinburgh or of England. Just the tops of the fence posts stick out of the snow. Follow them along the ridge for an hour or two, and find yourself looking down into one of the Southern Upland glens. But even then, it's just an icy river far below and a strip of empty roadway, with a silence as deep as when the Stewart kings cleared this ground for deer hunting, or the Armstrongs from over the hill drove away the cattle, burned the small thatched cottages and left a huddle of spear-slain corpses at the field corner.

*Loch Enoch, Rhinns of Kells from Redstone Rig (Walk 5)*

The Southern Uplands under snow are as big and blank as the screen before an outdoor movie show. What sort of story is going to unfold across the empty whiteness? A romance of the lonesome explorer high in the cold blue air; a grim epic of thigh-deep struggles in the white-out; or perhaps some frivolous bit of fun involving snowballs and an evening mince pie at the Tibbie Shiels Inn.

## ROLLING – BUT ALSO ROCKY

Like Yosemite's granite or Snowdonia's volcanics, the main range of the Southern Uplands is made of one sort of stone. It's the deep-ocean sludge called greywacke that gives the chunky dry-stone walls, the occasional blocky outcrops, the scaurs (slopes stripped to scree and bare rock) and the cleuchs (deep-cut little stream valleys).

These hills have their rocky moments, but moments only – small stream gullies, broken slopes of stone and scree. But in between the long, rambling days across the grassy tops, short but strenuous half days lead up the small rocky outliers with the big views – Eildon and North Berwick Law; pink Tinto, whose stones colour the roads of Lanarkshire; and seaside Screel, looking across the Solway to England's Lake District.

And away in the west is something even better.

Here is where the uniform greywacke of the main Southern Uplands is suddenly broken. The grim granite country of the Merrick is unlike anywhere else in the UK. Slabs of bare

*Basalt on the Girvan shoreline, looking over to the volcanic plug of Ailsa Craig (Walk 2)*

rock give easy walking across the humps of the Dungeon Hills – easy walking until the granite ends at knee-deep tussocks or a swamp of black peat. A wild goat stands on the skyline, and all below you are silver lochans trapped in the hollows of the rock.

<h2>LISTS OF HILLS</h2>

The Scottish Highlands are dominated by their list of the 282 Munros, the mountains rising above the 3000ft (or 914.4m) mark.

Southern Scotland has none of these. The next category down are called Corbetts. These are hills of 2500ft (762m), with the added requirement of having a clear drop around them of 500ft (152m). The Southern Uplands can boast seven: Merrick, Corserine, Shalloch on Minnoch and Cairnsmore (Section 1 of this book); Hart Fell and White Coomb (Section 3); and Broad Law (Section 4). Add an eighth when we count in the Cheviot, just a few miles into England in this book's Section 6.

However, the hill list specific to Southern Scotland is the one compiled by Percy Donald in 1935. The 140 Donalds are all over 2000ft (610m) high, but the drop around each can be as little as 50ft (15m) if the hill has 'topographic merit'. Donald distinguished between 'hills' (current surveys give 89 of these) and less significant 'tops' (currently 51) – but anyone going after this lot generally ticks them all.

The final listing to consider is the so-called Marilyns. These are hills, however low or high, that have a clear drop of 150m around them. Thus all Corbetts are by definition Marilyns. But so are lowly Grey Hill at Girvan (Walk 1) and Arthur's Seat (Walk 34). The Southern Uplands' incised valleys create a grand number of Marilyns – at the foot of Ettrick glen one could get five of them in a day.

Magnificent Marilyns, which might otherwise be ignored because of being below the arbitrary 2000ft or 600m mark, include Ailsa Craig (Walk 2), Criffel above the Solway (Walk 11), Well Hill at Durisdeer (Walk 13) and the Broughton Heights (three of them on Walk 17). Ward Law (Walk 23) and the Wiss (Walk 24) both overlook St Mary's Loch in the Yarrow Valley. Over in the east, the Marilyn listing takes in the Tweed with Rubers Law (Walk 32) and Eildon (Walk 31), celebrates the Pentlands (two of them on Walk 33), and lingers over little North Berwick Law (Walk 38). These range in height from 606m down to a mere 187m.

Such lists can act as a spur to further hill-going, and take walkers to places they wouldn't otherwise think of. (Even if, in the event, some of those places turn out to be only moderately attractive.) This book concentrates on the most worthwhile summits, irrespective of altitudes and listings – so that even one of the Corbetts (Shalloch on Minnoch of Galloway) is ignored in favour of lowly (but lovely) Screel Hill above the Solway.

## BORDER REIVERS

For 300 years, between the Battle of Bannockburn and the union of the Scottish and English crowns in 1604, the Border was an enclave between the two countries where neither king really ruled. Anarchy and lawlessness were convenient for London and Edinburgh as a buffer between the two kingdoms. But for those who lived there, it meant starvation or death by the spear. Family and the local warlord were all that stood between you and the raiders from England – or the Scottish warlord in the next-door glen.

From Nithsdale in Dumfriesshire to Redesdale and the North Tyne, the Border had its own laws, its own ethics, and an economy based on theft, blackmail and kidnapping for ransom. Over moorland and bog, through the passes of Cheviot and the fords of the Tyne, reivers rode up to 60 miles in an autumn night. After a skirmish at dawn with lances and the long-shafted Jedburgh axe they would ride back again with stolen cows, leaving the smoke of burning thatch behind them.

The most feared clans on the Scottish side of the border were the Armstrongs, Elliots, Scotts and Kerrs; on the English, the Grahams, Fenwicks and Forsters. The author's Turnbull ancestors were a small but effective gang inhabiting Teviotdale. (See whether your ancestors were involved by searching online for 'reiver surnames'.)

A record of those times is found in the Border ballads collected by Sir Walter Scott 200 years after the event. But they live on also in the defensive pele towers still standing above empty fields. Smaller fortified farms called bastles are in England only; the Scots ones were all destroyed. 'Thieves' roads' still run across the hilltops. Horseback 'march ridings' re-enact the battles around the stout, rugby-playing Border towns that stood through the anarchy. And the Border's harsh history is shown in the emptiness, even today, of the green glens that run south to the Tyne and northwards to the Tweed.

## THE COVENANTERS

In the times up to and including the English Civil War, Scotland developed its own Presbyterian form of Protestant religion – one in which spiritual leaders were democratically elected by a Presbytery council of church members. After the restoration of the monarchy in 1660 Charles II re-imposed bishops, and with them the king's authority over the church. Those who rejected king and bishops in Scotland were known as Covenanters. Often they held their illegal church services ('conventicles') in remote hollows of the hills.

Covenanters were at their strongest in Galloway, Ayrshire and Dumfriesshire. In 1667 their small army of rebellion marched on Edinburgh and was defeated at Rullion Green in the Pentlands. This marked the start of the Killing Times, when redcoats recruited from the Highlands broke up conventicles with muskets, and arrested, interrogated and tortured locals. Anyone too slow in renouncing their Protestant extremism went to Edinburgh for hanging in Greyfriars kirkyard or, in less serious cases, for transportation to the plantations of the West Indies. The victims responded with what today would be called terrorist attacks, such as the murder in 1677 of the Archbishop of St Andrews. Both sides believed that any cruelties were entirely justified as they had God entirely on their side, while their opponents belonged to Satan.

In 1688 James II (James VII of Scotland) was thrown out of England. The replacement joint monarchs, William and Mary of Orange, were moderate Protestants, and the Killing Times thus came to an end. The Covenanters were in effect the winners – the Church of Scotland is still Presbyterian. Accordingly, the Covenanting victims of the persecution became 'martyrs', whose stone memorials are in churchyards and on hillsides all over the Southern Uplands.

For further information on the covenanters see the website 'jardine's book of martyrs' (http://drmarkjardine. wordpress.com).

## WHEN TO GO

With a maximum altitude of 843m and few fearsome cliffs to fall off, the Southern Uplands can be enjoyed at any time of the year. As on most UK hills, the very best months are usually April to June, when the air is cool and clear, and rainfall is lower than in other seasons.

Wee Queensberry (Walk 12) looking across Nithsdale to the Galloway Hills

In high summer, July and August, the hills are slightly busier, although even then they are far from crowded. The grassland is a duller green, and the air is warm and hazy. Long days allow you to imitate, if you wish, the tremendous hill crossings of the Border reivers, and quiet summer evenings can be every bit as lovely as the crisp-ness of spring. Midges do haunt the wooded glens, with Glentrool below the Merrick and Kielder Forest in Northumberland being as afflicted as anywhere in the Scottish Highlands. However, open hill slopes and farm-land glens are usually midge free.

Autumn weather can be tiresome, with occasional brisk, windswept hill days sparkling within weeks of grey rain like the hill lochs among the Galloway bog. As the range stretches from coast to coast, one end may well have better weather than the other. However, the lack of roads and through-routes doesn't aid any last-minute shift from New Galloway to North Berwick.

Winter hill-walking here can be a special experience, with its huge and solitary empty spaces. But snow cover is unreliable. Some winters are almost snow free. Others fail to achieve any freeze–thaw cycle, with deep drifts that will rarely have been trodden down by any earlier walkers. In the occasional years when it comes into condition, the Grey Mare's Tail (see Walk 21) has ice-climbers queuing into the night for its frozen splendours. The steep north and east faces of Merrick can be a crampon-wearer's playground, with some actual winter climbs in the Black Gairy crags. But while revisiting the walks in this book, my best winter day just happened to be in the small-scale Pentlands (Walk 33).

The **Mountain Weather Information Service** provides daily forecasts for the Scottish, English and Welsh mountains. It happens to be based in Galloway's Glenkens, so its specific 'Southern Uplands' forecast is no afterthought, but at least as care-fully prepared as those for higher and busier bits of hill elsewhere. See www.mwis.org.uk.

## TRANSPORT

The Southern Uplands are approached by way of Glasgow, Edinburgh or Carlisle. Air travellers could touch down at Glasgow and Edinburgh, as well as Prestwick or Newcastle. Within the area, the main trans-port hubs are Dumfries, Galashiels, Hawick and Berwick-upon-Tweed. Few local buses are helpful to hill-walkers; convenient car hire is at Carlisle, Dumfries and Berwick.

For general information on transport in Scotland, contact www.travelinescotland.com, 0871 200 2233. Details of local transport, by area, are given in Appendix B.

### Rail

Both East Coast and West Coast main lines pass through the Southern Uplands, but their former stations among the hills have closed. Only the side line Dumfries–Glasgow has useful stations on it (for Section 2 of the guide). For more details contact www.scotrail.co.uk.

## Bus and coach

The main towns have useful bus services (with long-distance routes to and from Newton Stewart). However, the minor A-roads and byways serving the hill-walker have infrequent buses or none at all. School bus services are absent at weekends and during school holidays. Main-road services stop at intermediate points only at the discretion of the driver.

This guide is designed to offer readers the area's best walks. However, not all these are accessible by public transport. Bus services that might be useful to walkers generally include the 101/102 Edinburgh–Dumfries via Thornhill/Moffat, which gives access to many Southern Upland walks (Stagecoach West Scotland, 01292 613500). This and other services are listed by area in Appendix B.

Where a walk in this guide has useful, regular public transport to within a mile or so of the start, this is noted in the information box at the start of the walk. This applies to Walks 1–3, 11, 13, 14, 27–29, 31–34, 38 and 39.

## ACCOMMODATION

The Borders Region is very well served with hotels and B&Bs, and they'll be found in all the small towns throughout this book. 'Country house hotels', aimed at fishing and shooting enthusiasts, are particularly comfortable (and expensive!) and are used to muddy boots and dogs. B&Bs on existing long-distance paths (Southern Upland Way, St Cuthbert's Way, Border Abbeys Way) are also walker-friendly and are listed on the paths' websites and accommodation leaflets.

## Hostels and bothies

The Scottish Youth Hostels Association (www.syha.org.uk) still runs a handful of hostels in the Borders; most are closed in winter. There are also a few independent hostels (www.hostel-scotland.co.uk). The area has many bothies – simple unlocked shelters with no facilities. They are occasionally unavailable during work parties or closed by vandalism; consult www.mountainbothies.org.uk.

Details of hostels and bothies in each area covered by the guide are given in Appendix B.

## TOURIST INFORMATION AND OTHER FACILITIES

For general information see www.visitscotland.com and www.discovertheborders.co.uk. Year-round information centres are located in Dumfries (01387 253862), Peebles (01721 723159) and at Princes Street, Edinburgh (0845 225 5121). Details of local tourist information contact points for each area covered by this guide are given in Appendix B.

The small towns of the area have been largely self-sufficient since the reiving times – they are well served with pubs, cafés, shops and petrol stations. A few parts of the area, such as the Galloway Hills, have no nearby town; for them, notes on local facilities are given in Appendix B.

## MAPS

The mapping in this guide is based on the Ordnance Survey's Landranger series at 1:50,000. However, anyone walking in the hills needs to be able to see a larger area of land than the small extracts on these pages, so as to be aware of escape routes and neighbouring glens (in case you come down the wrong side of the hill). It is recommended that walkers take with them a paper map sheet (or electronic equivalent).

The 1:50,000 Landranger mapping covers the area of this guide on sheets 66 (Edinburgh), 67 (Duns), 72* (Upper Clyde), 73* (Peebles), 74* (Kelso), 76 (Girvan), 77* (Dalmellington), 78* (Nithsdale), 79* (Hawick), 80* (Cheviot Hills), 83 (Newton Stewart) and 84 (Dumfries), with the starred sheet numbers being more important.

The area is also covered on the OS Explorer maps at 1:25,000 scale. Their main advantage is in showing fences and walls, along with much extra detail in the valleys. Against this, they are bulkier than the Landranger maps and considerably less clear to read. Refer to the box at the start of individual walks for the relevant sheet numbers.

While either scale of Ordnance Survey mapping is good, the mapping by Harveys is even better on the ground that they cover. Their maps are specifically designed for walkers and are beautifully clear and legible, mark paths where they actually exist on the ground, and do not disintegrate when damp. Their 1:25,000 Superwalker 'Galloway Hills' covers the main range, but not Cairnsmore of Fleet; the 1:40,000 Superwalker 'Cheviot Hills' covers the book's three final routes. Harveys have also mapped the Pentlands and Edinburgh. If a Harveys map is available, details are given in the box at the start of the walk.

## COMPASS AND GPS

A compass is a very useful aid in mist, even if your skills only extend to 'northwest, southeast' rather than precision bearings. Magnetic deviation is about 4° west. This can often be ignored; otherwise, to convert a map bearing to a compass one, add 4. GPS receivers should be set to the British National Grid (known variously as British Grid, Ord Srvy GB, BNG, or OSGB GRB36).

## SAFETY IN THE MOUNTAINS

Safety and navigation in the mountains are best learnt from companions, experience and perhaps a paid instructor; such instruction is outside

*Grouse-shooters' tracks, such as this one below Garroch Fell (Walk 12), often give easy going between the hills*

the scope of this book. For those experienced in Snowdonia or the Lake District, these hills are easier going, but can be a lot more remote.

The international mountain distress signal is some sign (shout, whistle, torch flash or other) repeated six times over a minute, followed by a minute's silence. The reply is a sign repeated three times over a minute, followed by a minute's silence. To signal for help from a helicopter, raise both arms above the head and then drop them down sideways, repeatedly. If you're not in trouble, don't shout or whistle on the hills, and don't wave to passing helicopters.

To call out the rescue services, phone 999 from a landline. From a mobile, phone either 999 or the international emergency number 112 – these will connect you via any available network. Reception is poor along the hilltops; at the hill edges, it's a matter of luck whether the stretch of glen you're looking down at has a phone mast. Sometimes a text message can get through when a voice call to the rescue service can't – pre-register your phone at www.emergencysms.org.uk.

### Avalanches

The Scottish Avalanche Information Service's website (www.sais.gov. uk) doesn't cover these less-frequented hills, but it and the fell-top report for the Lake District (www. lakedistrictweatherline.co.uk) can give general indications of conditions. Snow build-up is usually less than in the Highlands, and slopes are not as steep. Even so, avalanches do happen.

The Ettrick hills – Capel Fell seen from Croft Head (Walk 19)

Greatest avalanche danger arises during heavy snowfall and for a couple of days afterwards on moderately steep slopes facing away from the wind. So after snowfall from the southwest, east- and north-facing slopes may be at risk.

### USING THIS GUIDE

Walks in the guide are grouped into six local areas. A box at the start of each walk summarises key information, including start/finish points, distance, ascent (and maximum altitude), maps and an estimated time for the walk. The box also gives details of the terrain, parking/facilities and any route variants. A summary of the walks appears in Appendix A to help you select the correct one for you and your party.

In the route description, a distinction is made between vertical and horizontal distance – '600m', for instance, indicates an altitude or height gain, and '600 metres' indicates distance along the ground. 'Track' (rather than 'path') refers to a way wide enough for a tractor or Landrover. Points of interest along the route are highlighted, and key navigational features that appear on the accompanying map are shown in **bold**.

Appendix B gives local information arranged by area, including tourist information, useful guidebooks and available facilities, including accommodation. Finally, a glossary of Scots terms in Appendix C should help you unravel some of the area's mysterious and poetic place names.

# 1 GALLOWAY

*Loch Enoch and Mullwarchar (Walk 6)*

# INTRODUCTION

Galloway is Scotland's southwest corner, bounded by the River Nith. It's a quiet, green country, whose bendy and bumpy country roads are good for cycling holidays. But for walkers, the heart of it is the hills around the Merrick, the summit of southern Scotland. And it feels like it – with its windy top, the longest view in the UK (you really can see Snowdon when the weather's just right), the ridge-line called Nieve of the Spit (Walk 5), and the super spur called Little Spear. But if 843m Merrick was tough, you're in for a shock when you get into the granite lands below – bog and bare granite underfoot, an eagle overhead, and ground that's 50 per cent water.

And what water! Loch Enoch – it's the Loch Avon of the Southern Uplands. It's 'Eskwater', supposing Lakeland's majestic Upper Eskdale had the lake it so richly deserves. In March the whooper swans stop off at Loch Enoch – when you're on your way north to Iceland in one mighty flap, nowhere else quite cuts it.

Acting the goat on the granite and bog? You're not alone – several dozen actual goats leap about on Craignaw and the Dungeon Hill (Walk 6). A bit defeated at the end of the day? You're in good company – Robert the Bruce gave the English a bad bashing in the woods above Loch Trool.

But before the rigours of the granite, the Ayrshire coast offers a gentle day out on some very odd rocks (Walk 1), and a boat trip halfway to Arran (Walk 2).

# WALK 1
*Girvan and Grey Hill*

| | |
|---|---|
| **Start/Finish** | Girvan, south end (NX 183 964) |
| **Distance** | 21km (13 miles) |
| **Ascent** | 750m (2500ft) |
| **Approx time** | 6½hrs |
| **Terrain** | Grassy hills, track, foreshore (rugged in places) |
| **Max altitude** | Grey Hill, 297m |
| **Maps** | Landranger 76 (Girvan); Explorer 317 (Ballantrae) |
| **Public transport** | Girvan station. Bus 54 (Girvan–Stranraer) stops at Lendalfoot to allow a linear walk. |
| **Parking** | Free car park with toilets and snack shack |

Walkers spend the morning high up, for the sea views; the afternoon along the coast path, for poking in the rock pools. Grey Hill is a perfect little ridgeline – grassy to walk, with outcrops of odd lumpy rock for decoration. Lurid gorse clashes with a vibrant blue sky. At the trig point, peculiar pink stones form a grassy nook to gaze out at the island of Ailsa Craig.

Ailsa Craig is the plug of a volcano that popped up at the opening of the Atlantic a mere 50 million years ago. As ancient rocks go, that's the day before yesterday. The pink rocks on Grey Hill are nearly ten times as ancient, and a whole lot odder. It's a defective granite called Trondhjemite, which properly belongs below the ocean bed.

The coastal path weaves between former sea stacks of a raised beach, then heads north on a grass track – and on Lendalfoot foreshore are some *really* odd rocks. The final 3km are harder going, along beaches of sand and pebbles.

Head inland along the A77 to a roundabout with a red sandstone centrepiece claiming Girvan as Home of Ailsa Craig. ▶ Go straight across into a housing estate. As the street bends left, keep ahead through a gate signed 'Girvan Barr hill path'. This track leads up past Piedmont house, over a railway, and through a bluebell wood.

Old Red Sandstone here and at the car park indicates that Girvan itself stands just north of the Southern Upland fault.

At the wood top is a small quarry. Here turn right, up open grassy slopes. Cross an ancient field system onto the hill fort summit of **Dow Hill**.

> The rock outcrops are a **puddingstone** (the Benan Conglomerate), containing large rounded cobbles. The basic grey is a greywacke-type sandstone, as found all across the Southern Uplands. The pink lumps within it are an alien rock, Trondhjemite, described below.

Head down southwest over an awkward fence (down right 100 metres to a field corner may help). Pass down to the right of a gorse grove to a gate and arch under the railway. A tractor track leads down to the A714. Cross and turn left along the pavement to a cemetery.
Turn right, forking left on a farm track.

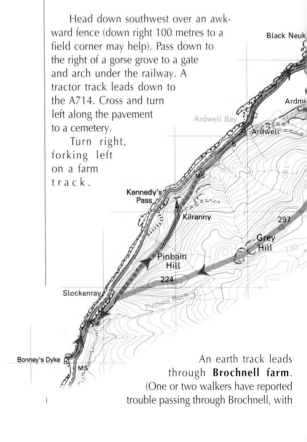

An earth track leads through **Brochnell farm**. (One or two walkers have reported trouble passing through Brochnell, with

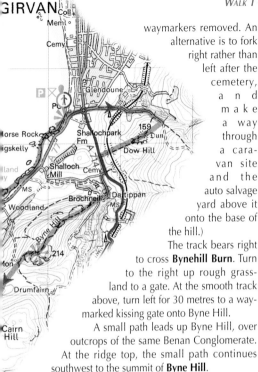

waymarkers removed. An alternative is to fork right rather than left after the cemetery, and make a way through a caravan site and the auto salvage yard above it onto the base of the hill.)

The track bears right to cross **Bynehill Burn**. Turn to the right up rough grassland to a gate. At the smooth track above, turn left for 30 metres to a way-marked kissing gate onto Byne Hill.

A small path leads up Byne Hill, over outcrops of the same Benan Conglomerate. At the ridge top, the small path continues southwest to the summit of **Byne Hill**.

The outcrops here are of pure **Trondhjemite**. It's a pink and crystalline granite, but without granite's back speckles. When exposed in outcrops it weathers to a dull grey – you'll see clean chunks of it along the foreshore at the walk's end.

The small path continues down southwest to a stile. Head down through a wall gate to cross a col. ▶ Ahead is a slightly rocky hummock (Mains Hill), made of massive greywacke. Cross its grassy top and continue on down through low gorse to cross a stream. Go through fallen stone sheepfolds to a gate, with a faint grass track

A stone monument, decomposed so that whatever it commemorates has fallen off, is over on the right.

27

*Up the north ridge of Grey Hill, with Byne Hill seen behind*

beyond. This runs up to the right of the stream, then leads up all the way to the trig point on **Grey Hill**.

The level summit section ends with a bit more Trondhjemite.

Continue southwest along the small ridge path. ◄ Cross a fence on the way down to a col, with a gate in a wall, and go up the slight rise of **Pinbain Hill**. Keep ahead down the southwest spur of Pinbain Hill through a gate in a fence to a gate and kissing gate, where a gravel track contours in from the right. There is now a choice – to turn sharp right immediately, or to continue down the Ayrshire Coast Path ahead to a beach for a lunch stop before returning to this point. ◄

Turning back here saves 2km (¾hr).

Ahead are **raised beaches** along the shoreline to Lendalfoot, with former sea stacks projecting from the (now grassy) meadows behind the main road. The old beach, now above sea level, shows how the west of Scotland has been rising steadily since the weight of the Ice Age melted off.

To continue on the Coast Path take the grass track ahead through the gate. It bends right, down through

## SERPENTINE

Just occasionally it happens that the crunching together of continents brings rocks from below the deep ocean floor right up to the surface. This has happened at two places in the UK – the Lizard in Cornwall and the Ayrshire coast between Girvan and Ballantrae.

*Serpentine from Bonney's Dyke*

One of the strange stones exposed is the pink Trondhjemite of Byne Hill. This is a primordial rock of the oceanic crust, formed at the mid-ocean ridge as the ocean on either side moved outwards. That rock is usually basalt, but can sometimes be Trondhjemite.

At Bonney's Dyke, the turning point of this walk, appears a stone from even further down. It's a gabbro, but with gabbro's usual black crystals separated by a groundmass of off-white feldspar. This rock originally crystallised below the ocean floor. On the beach at Bonney's Dyke are occasional dark, streaked pebbles, coloured greenish, reddish or yellow and slippery to the touch. This comes from even lower still. It's the stone called serpentine (strictly, serpentinite), which is not from the earth's crust at all but is from the next layer down, the mantle, 10km or more below the ocean floor.

The serpentinite rock forms cliffs at Balcreuchan Port, 5km south down the coast. It overhangs a cave once lurked in by the cannibal family of Sawney Bean.

what appears to be a quarry (actually a former sea cove with sea stacks). Cross the **A77** and turn left along the pavement for 700 metres to a lay-by, above a cluster of beach rocks projecting seawards – **Bonney's Dyke**.

Return alongside the A77 and up the grassy track. Once through the second gate, the track continues gravel surfaced, contouring below a mobile phone mast. The track crosses the steep hillside to **Kilranny** ruin. Here a kissing gate on the left lets walkers bypass the former farmyard and rejoin the track through another kissing gate beyond.

*Bonney's Dyke to Pinbain Hill – the foreground rocks are speckled gabbro*

The track now runs gently downhill to sea level. Where it bends left across the green meadow of the raised beach (to the A77 just ahead), keep ahead (Ayrshire Coast Path waymark here, below strikingly folded greywacke rock). A rougher track passes along the inland edge of the raised beach. Just before **Ardwell farm**, turn down left to cross the A77 to a pathway signpost.

Follow the road verge for 300 metres, with folded greywacke rocks offering a very rugged alternative along the shoreline. As the road bends left it is possible to drop left onto the beach (unless the tide is fully in). Walk along the beach back to the walk start.

# WALK 2
*Ailsa Craig*

| | |
|---|---|
| **Start/Finish** | Girvan harbour (NX 184 981) |
| **Distance** | 2.5km (1½ miles) |
| **Ascent** | 340m (1110ft) |
| **Approx time** | 2hrs |
| **Terrain** | Steep path |
| **Max altitude** | Ailsa Craig, 338m |
| **Maps** | Landranger 76 (Girvan); Explorer 317 (Ballantrae) |
| **Public transport** | Girvan station |
| **Access** | The author crossed with established boatman Mark McCrindle (www.ailsacraig.org.uk) |
| **Parking** | Street parking near harbour |

Ailsa Craig is the only island in the world with a variety of onion named after it. And just like an onion it can make you cry – not because of the awkward journey to Girvan and the slightly pricey boat trip, but because even if you extravagantly booked for 3 hours on the island, when it's time for the boat you haven't been there nearly long enough.

The boatman will take you right around the island before landing at the pier. Poisoning of the island's rats has allowed the ground-nesting puffins to recover, while there have always been gulls, gannets and everything else that goes squawk and drops a splat onto the deck beside you. Bring binoculars and a splat-proof hat.

The ascent of the island is straightforward, if strenuous. From the pier, head across the island's small patch of level ground onto a path that slants steeply up left. It zigzags back right to reach the ruined **Castle of Ailsa**, perched a third of the way up the slope.

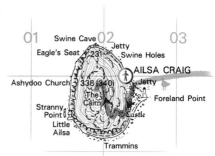

*Ailsa Craig north end, with remains of a foghorn tower*

Gulls nest alongside the path as it slants up to the right, working up the eastern slope of the island then straight uphill to the trig point, with its magnificent view.

If the **summit** is in cloud, a compass bearing is useful to ensure you head down the correct slope. Directions other than east lead to a lot of seagulls and possibly a messy and dung-smeared death.

Return down the small path to the cottages near the pier.

A former tramway along the shoreline allows a strangely horizontal walk towards either of the massive abandoned foghorns seen from the cruise around the island.

# WALK 3

*Cairnsmore of Fleet*

| | |
|---|---|
| **Start/Finish** | Cairnsmore Hill car park (NX 463 632) |
| **Distance** | 14.5km (9 miles) |
| **Ascent** | 750m (2500ft) |
| **Approx time** | 5¼hrs |
| **Terrain** | Hill path, rough grassy plateau and slope, moorland track |
| **Max altitude** | Cairnsmore of Fleet, 711m |
| **Maps** | Landranger 83 (Newton Stewart); Explorer 319 (Galloway S) |
| **Public transport** | Bus 500/X75 (Dumfries–Stranraer) stops at Palnure |
| **Parking** | Turn off A75 at Muirfad, 800 metres east of Palnure. The minor road bends left across a stream and between piers of a former rail bridge. Ahead 300 metres is a 'P' sign – parking is in the disused track on the right. |

Cairnsmore of Fleet is the southernmost 2000ft (600m) summit in Scotland, and its isolated position above the Solway Firth explains its wide views, and also the memorial to crashed aeroplanes at the summit. Cairnsmore is also a high-altitude bog of national importance. However, that area – with granite and peat as austere as Craignaw (Walk 6) – lies to the north of the summit. This gentler route is on comfortable grass, with a mysterious old path (perhaps formed by peat cutters) zigzagging up the wide slope above the lowlands of the Cree.

After the pleasant plateau wander, the descent is rather more rugged, with some granite boulder-fields to weave around. But at the slope foot another old track leads conveniently across the moor back to Cairnsmore farm.

Continue up the track and through a little iron gate onto the driveway towards Cairnsmore farm. Keep ahead for 1km up the estate track. At the first buildings bear right on the main track, then turn right at a small sign on a path through rhododendron and laurel. At a higher track turn left, and continue to its end above **Cairnsmore farm**.

*Cairnsmore of Fleet, seen across the Cree estuary*

Take the gate ahead, and bear right up a field to a gate at its top left corner. A clear path runs uphill through plantations. At a signed junction, keep ahead, signposted for Cairnsmore summit.

The path crosses a track (stone bench here), then emerges onto open hill and crosses a ladder stile. It runs uphill to pass through a gap in a fallen granite wall, above which it zigzags quite steeply up. As the slope eases, the path is less visible but is marked by cairns. At one of these cairns it bends left, north, passing a memorial to airmen just before the trig point and shelter cairn at **Cairnsmore** summit.

Three peaks hereabouts are 'Cairnsmore'; the others are of Carsphairn (Walk 8) and of Dee, which is densely planted and not an attractive walk. All three of them are **granite hills**. The name, meaning 'large stone-pile hill', may refer not to their height but to their sprawling granite-hill shapes.

Turn southeast down the gently

sloping summit plateau, soon with cliffs dropping to the left. Posts of a former fence guide down to a col (Nick of Clashneach), where the route passes through a gap in an old wall. Head uphill, southeast, and at the slope top turn south along the level plateau. At its far end is the large, ancient cairn of **Knee of Cairnsmore**.

Descend southwest over grassy ground on a vague spur-line. As the ground steepens, find a grassy way down between granite boulder-fields. Cross the head of a shallow stream hollow onto the moorland beyond, named as **Knocktim**. Turn southwest along the crest of this on short mossy heather, and after 400 metres or so join a faint old track. ▶

At the tip of Knocktim (NX 497 634) the track bends right, west. It

This track appears on modern Explorer maps and old Landrangers.

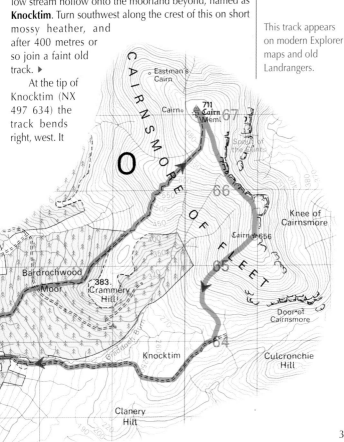

*Looking west from Craignelder, in the rough plateau northwards from Cairnsmore of Fleet*

runs down rough peaty pasture, becoming a stony farm track and joining **Graddoch Burn**, with forest plantations opposite. The track runs down to a gate, where it fades into a field. Head down the right edge next to the stream to another gate. Through this, the track continues down to the left of the stream, across it at a bridge with 5 ton weight limit, and continues downhill, now to the right of the stream, to a track T-junction near a house.

Turn right, and in about 150 metres turn down left in the laurel-wood path you arrived on. Follow the track below Cairnsmore farm back to the car park.

# WALK 4
## *Minnigaff Hills*

| | |
|---|---|
| **Start/Finish** | Auchenleck Bridge, 6km northeast of Newton Stewart (NX 447 705) |
| **Distance** | 21km (13 miles) |
| **Ascent** | 1300m (4300ft) |
| **Approx time** | 8hrs |
| **Terrain** | Forest roads, grassy hill ridges; pathless slopes of grass and short heather; rough forest ride near walk start, and fairly rough descent from Curleywee |
| **Max altitude** | Lamachan Hill, 717m |
| **Maps** | Landranger 77 (Dalmellington); Explorer 319 (Galloway S); Harveys Galloway Hills (omits tracks at start and end) |
| **Parking** | Roadside pull-in at forest road end beside Auchenleck bridge |

The Minnigaff Hills may be small, but they're as shaggy and wild as the mountain goats that roam over them. The approach from the south makes sure the northward view of the Merrick and its surrounding lochs socks you in the eye as you reach the ridgeline. And it gives a natural horseshoe to compare and contrast all four Minnigaff summits.

Larg is gently grassy – it'll mislead you into thinking the walk ahead will be an easy one. Lamachan, too, is grassy, but leads into a knobbly ridgeline, excitingly bypassed by a path across the top of the northern slope. That path is narrow and slightly rocky, and was made in the first place by goats.

Curleywee is just as nice as its name. Thread up among scree and small crags to the grassy hollow at its top. This is southwest Scotland, so you'll have that top to yourself. The route threads down among more small crags onto a moorland of orange grasses and a dozen sky-coloured lochans. For your fourth hill, massive, sprawling Millfore is heathery to start with, past the peaty little Black Loch. It's grassy above, past the high-cupped White Lochan; and the descent over Drigmorn offers the third hilltop lochan, frillingly named as Fuffock.

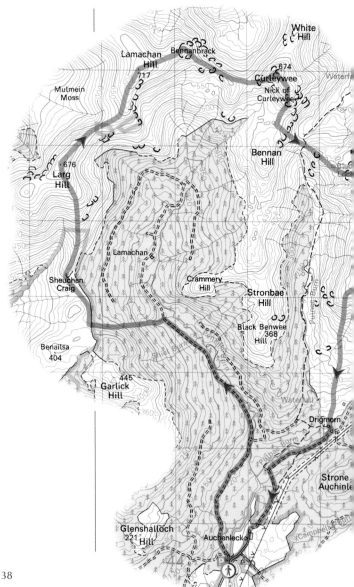

Take the forest road running northwest. After 1km it runs alongside **Penkiln Burn**. In another 2km the ground up left has newly planted trees, and views open ahead to show Larg Hill. The track crosses a first small concrete bridge, and in 500 metres more it crosses a second one and is about to re-enter trees.

Turn up left, alongside the tree edge and Benroach Burn. After 300 metres the right-hand (north) bank is obstructed by windblown trees. Cross to the awkward rough ground on the left side of the stream. Just above, a clear gap continues uphill, east. (The gap separates young trees on the right from newly planted trees on the left.)

The ride arrives at the wall at the plantation top, south of Sheuchanower. Turn north, with the wall on your right, across Sheuchanower's slight rise, then up the grassy slope towards Larg Hill. ▸ At a wall junction, keep ahead to the summit cairn on **Larg Hill**.

Here, at the natural treeline, scrubby dwarf pine has been left to itself on the slope to your right.

*Larg Hill from the slopes of Lamachan (granite erratic boulder in the foreground)*

The col is a small meltwater channel, from when ice filled the Loch Trool valley on your left. That same glacier has dumped granite boulders along the ridge.

Head northeast, to the left of another wall, down to Nick of the Brushy. ◀ A small path leads up **Lamachan Hill**. The summit is marked by a gateway gap in a falling stone wall.

Head roughly northeast across the plateau, following occasional old iron fence posts, to **Bennanbrack**. Now descend southeast on a lumpy ridge. Look out for the small goat path just down on the left; it takes an exciting line just below the ridge crest.

After Nick of Corners Gate, the goat path contours across the north side of a hump called Milldown to arrive in **Nick of Curleywee**. Go through a wall gap and head up the steep face of **Curleywee**.

Descend Curleywee with care. Head southeast across a slight col, over the spur top of Gaharn, and gently down for another 50 metres or so. Now turn down right to descend slightly west of south, weaving between rocky bits of ground, onto a flat moorland. Cross this towards **Bennan Hill** to find a falling stone wall. Turn left down this, with a path. Keep downhill through a fence gate to Loup of Laggan pass.

Cross the path that passes through the pass and head up the lumpy moorland ridge opposite, keeping to the

*Curleywee on the approach from Nick of Curleywee*

highest line. Pass **Black Loch** (small, among heather) and then **White Lochan** (larger, among grass). Now find a faint quad-bike track along the grassy ridgeline. There's a slight dip, then a grassy rise to the summit ridge of Millfore. Turn left to the **Millfore** summit trig.

Return along the summit ridge, past Millfore's south-west top. A quad-bike track runs down past the lochan called Fuffock on **Drigmorn Hill**.

**Fuffock**: one of the flat tassels in the dimples of an old mattress? A person who, at any stop, takes every single item out of their rucksack?

Continue briefly down southwest until the ridgeline steepens. Now turn left off the quad-bike trail to descend south, following the highest ground midway between Pulnee and Green Burns.

As the slope eases, with luck another quad-bike path will be found, which leads into fields. If it arrives at a fence gate, move left for 100 metres to a wall gateway near a little black shed. Pass through a second gateway, where a track runs ahead to an abandoned cottage, **Drigmorn**. ▶

Behind the house the track fords **Green Burn**. Turn right on the forest road beyond. It runs downvalley past **Auchenleck** to the walk start.

On old Landranger maps this name, Drigmorn, is 500 metres too far north.

# WALK 5

*Merrick and Murder Hole*

| | |
|---|---|
| **Start/Finish** | Lower car park at Bruce's Stone (NX 414 803) |
| **Distance** | 14.5km (9 miles) |
| **Ascent** | 700m (2700ft) |
| **Approx time** | 5½hrs |
| **Terrain** | Good path up Merrick, then grassy descent and small rough paths that can be peaty and wet |
| **Max altitude** | Merrick, 843m |
| **Maps** | Landranger 77 (Dalmellington); Explorer 318 (Galloway N); Harveys Galloway Hills |
| **Parking** | The lower Bruce's Stone car park, with a 'dual carriageway' layout |
| **Variants** | Ascent via Fell of Eschoncan (no extra distance or mileage but a lot rougher); descent by Rig of the Buchan (described in Walk 6) – 13.5km (8½ miles) with 900m (3000ft) of ascent (about 5hrs) |

The granite country of Galloway is southern Scotland's lakeland, with a score of lochs in an area just 30km across. This lochan-wander takes in four of the best – Trool, Valley, Neldricken and the highest and wildest water south of the Highlands, Loch Enoch. Almost as an afterthought Merrick is thrown in, the highest of the Southern Upland hills (but not the wildest – that's Craignaw, on Walk 6).

And the Murder Hole? It's a pool of unwholesome reeds and black water at the corner of Loch Neldricken. It's bottomless and never freezes over, and it's where the bog brigands of 200 years ago used to fling the unwanted carcasses of their victims. At least, if you believe *The Raiders*, by SR Crockett – a friend of Robert Louis Stevenson and almost his equal when it comes to a hill-walking adventure story to tingle your boot soles.

The alternative descent from Loch Enoch, by the Rig of the Buchan, is probably even nicer than the three lochs, while also being easier and drier underfoot. So if Merrick is to be your only route in Galloway, you may prefer to switch at Loch Enoch to this alternative descent.

## Diversion to Fell of Eschoncan

Near the top end of the car park a small bracken path heads up the steep side of Fell of Eschoncan – it was created with a strimmer for the first running of the Merrick hill race, but persists as a rugged alternative route over **Fell of Eschoncan**. The faint path then passes across the rough plateau of **Bennan**, staying below, and east of, the radio masts to continue north across a sometimes soggy wide col to join the main path up **Benyellary**.

Continue up the road beyond the lower car park for 10 metres, then take a small informal path through woods on its right. After 150 metres this arrives at Bruce's Stone, perched high above Loch Trool.

> **Bruce's Stone** is a granite erratic – a smaller but similar granite lump is nearby alongside the arrival path. The bedrock below the monument is grey-wacke sandstone, darker than the granite, here with the knobbly 'hornfelsed' texture – it has been cooked by the heat of the granite intrusion, whose edge is only a few hundred metres away. So the glacier has not had to bring the Bruce's boulder very far. However, some Galloway granite is found hundreds of miles away to the south and southeast.

*Merrick from the east – Redstone Rig runs down the left-hand skyline*

43

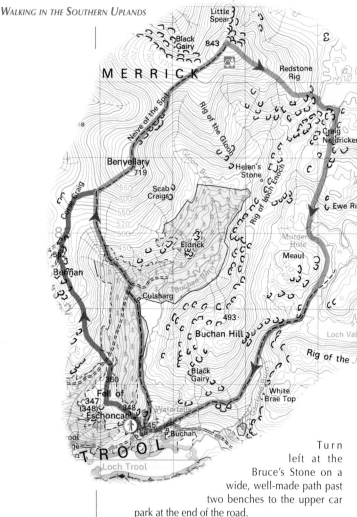

Turn left at the Bruce's Stone on a wide, well-made path past two benches to the upper car park at the end of the road.

At the top end of this upper car park a wide path sets off uphill (northeast), with a large signboard announcing it as the Merrick Trail. The path is rugged, with peat and boulders – it gets much better higher up. In 200 metres it arrives above the wooded slot of the **Buchan Burn**, with waterfalls heard below.

After running for 400 metres above the stream, the path turns uphill a little and contours through mature plantation. It is now wide and smooth and will remain so for the rest of the ascent. At **Culsharg** bothy the path turns uphill to a forest road. ▶ Turn right for 50 metres, crossing a stream, to find the path continuing uphill to the right of the stream. It emerges over a carved stone marking the top of woodland to pass through a gate on open hillside and then reach the wall up the southwest flank of Benyellary. The path runs up to the right of the wall to the large cairn on **Benyellary**.

Here the wall and path bend left, descending around the rim of the Gloon corrie onto the well-defined ridge-line of **Neive of the Spit**. The path to the right of the wall follows the very brink of the corrie; the one up to the left offers additional views westwards towards the sea and Ailsa Craig. At the end of this connecting ridge the

The bothy has recently been restored with glass windows and midgeproof door.

## GRANITE AND GREYWACKE

*Just above the granite junction on Redstone Rig*

The granite of the Galloway Highlands melted its way up into the standard Southern Upland rock, which is the chunky deep-ocean sandstone called greywacke. Around the edges of the granite the country rock is cooked and crumbled, so all around Mullwarchar and Craignaw lie valleys such as the Silver Flowe. But a mile or two further out, the surrounding greywacke was baked and hardened, and this tougher rock rises in the hill ridges of Merrick and the Kells and Minnigaffs. The result is a 'metamorphic areole', also known as 50 miles of fine hill-walking in a ring around the granite heartland.

The difference between the Merrick's greywacke and the granite around Loch Enoch is fairly noticeable as you descend Redstone Rig. Dark, uniform grey gives way to paler speckles; layered sandstone gives way to rounded granite. To inspect the actual rock junction, take a leftward line down the ridge and look for a striking slab sloped towards you. The granite–greywacke junction crosses the downhill rockface below (NX 4343 8532).

Approaching the granite, the heated greywacke loses its bedding structure. On the other side, approaching the magma chamber wall the granite forms only the smallest crystals, so the visible speckles are lost. Thus the difference between the two is less marked at the actual junction than across the hill as a whole.

wall and path bend slightly left (north) up the summit slope of Merrick. After 200 metres the path bends right, away from the wall, to rake up the hill flank to the white-painted trig point on **Merrick**.

Descend south of east, with steep drops into Howe of the Caldron on your left. In clear conditions, once at the plateau edge it is possible to see Loch Enoch spread below; head for its right-hand corner. In mist, the wide, lumpy **Redstone Rig** provides no clear line – aim somewhat to the left (north) of the loch corner, and on reaching the loch turn right along a sketchy path. The loch's southwest corner has a fence line running down to a tiny golden-sand beach. ◄

Continue along the loch's south side on a sketchy path for 250 metres, then turn up to the right into a grassy gap between two hillocks. At once this becomes a little pass, just 15m higher up than the loch itself. ◄

A peaty path forms in the little pass and leads down just west of south, with a small stream on its left, to reach the reed-infested western corner of Loch Neldricken, known as the **Murder Hole**.

Like Doone valley on Exmoor, the **Murder Hole** is a fictional place that has made it onto modern maps.

Here switch to Walk 6 for the Rig of Buchan descent.

The actual outflow is at the northwest corner, but here, and also the northeast and southeast corners, are almost outflows too.

In *The Raiders* by SR Crockett, the evil Macaterick bandits murdered passing hill-walkers for our sandwich snacks then trampled our bodies into the bog. Old postcards show it as an oval enclosure quite separate from the main lake.

*Merrick path, looking back along Neive of Spit to Benyellary*

Once past the soggy hollow put to such grim use by the fictitious (but very vicious) Macaterick clan, the path bends southeast across a flank of Meaul to reach the corner of **Loch Valley**. It runs along the loch's western end, then down beside its outflow, the **Gairland Burn**. ▶

The path here can become very soggy; an alternative path is to the left of the stream.

After 1km down the high hidden valley, the path contours out to the right – a 'seat stone' is alongside the stream here. The path, of peat puddles and tall rounded boulders, is tiring in descent. After passing behind a knoll there's a view of **Loch Trool** ahead, and the path slants down through bracken to the track running through the woods beside the loch.

Follow the track ahead, past **Buchan farm**, with its conical turret almost buried among the oaks, and across Buchan Burn below a waterfall. Where the uphill track bends right, take a small path ahead. The peat has eroded away to bare rock on the short pull up to Bruce's Stone.

# WALK 6

*The Dungeon Hills*

| | |
|---|---|
| **Start/Finish** | Lower car park at Bruce's Stone (NX 414 803) |
| **Distance** | 19km (12 miles) |
| **Ascent** | 1050m (3500ft) |
| **Approx time** | 7–8hrs |
| **Terrain** | Small rough paths, rough grassy hillsides and bare granite slabs |
| **Max altitude** | Mullwarchar, 692m |
| **Maps** | Landranger 77 (Dalmellington); Explorer 318 (Galloway N); Harveys Galloway Hills |
| **Parking** | The lower Bruce's Stone car park, with a 'dual carriageway' layout |
| **Variant** | Omit all three hills for a good bad-weather outing or short day past Lochs Valley and Neldricken to Galloway's central mystery, lovely Loch Enoch – 11.5km (7 miles) with 600m (2000ft) of ascent (about 4½hrs) |

Three ridges around the edge of the Galloway Hills include Merrick, Shalloch and Corserine, all with Corbett (2000-footer) status. But these ridges, like the Sanctuary around Annapurna, only conceal the inner hills – Craignaw, Mullwarchar and the Dungeon – and their unique little land of granite and standing water.

The land is home to grey mists, black peat and a herd of shaggy mountain goats, as well as the Murder Hole at the end of Loch Neldricken. There could have been an even more murderous hole in the middle of Mullwarchar, where it was planned to deposit nuclear waste hoping protesters wouldn't even be able to pronounce it. The Devil's Bowling Green, with balls as big as sheep, is a 'green' that's actually granite. And there's a special secret – high, wild Loch Enoch has an island, and that island itself contains a very small loch.

As the clouds descend onto the peaty holes and the rock slabs, in no time at all you're a lost walker. A lost walker within a (misty) mystery, wrapped within a secret, inside 30km of lochans and bog...

Continue up the road beyond the lower car park for 10 metres, then take a small informal path through woods

on its right. After 150 metres this arrives at Bruce's Stone, perched high above Loch Trool.

*Loch Valley outflow*

Keep ahead towards the loch head to find a small descending path where the peat is eroded down to bare rock. It joins a track descending from the car park to cross a bridge over **Buchan Burn**, then pass **Buchan house**. After 250 metres take a field gate on the left, with a sign-board for Loch Valley, for the start of a rough path.

The path slants up through bracken, then curves round into the valley of the **Gairland Burn**. Where it arrives beside the burn, there's a comfortable 'seat stone' beside the stream. The path runs up to the left of the burn to arrive at the outflow of Loch Valley. It passes to the left of **Loch Valley**, rather soft and wet. The path here is divided, with the left-hand and slightly higher branch eventually bearing up left to the **Murder Hole**. ▶

The Murder Hole is described in Walk 5.

### Short-cut – the three lochs

Even without the three Dungeon Hills, any visit to Loch Enoch is a rugged and rewarding hill day. ▶ At the corner of Loch Valley, take the more obvious path ahead, about 200 metres to the left of Mid Burn. It bends left as it rises around the flank of Meaul, then joins **Loch Neldricken** at its southwest corner (the **Murder Hole**).

This direct way to Loch Enoch reverses part of Walk 5.

Head around the loch corner, crossing a stream, then follow the path up in a straight line, just east of north, with a small stream on its right. Loch Arron is just visible on your right, then the path passes through a tiny grassy pass for the very slight drop to **Loch Enoch**.

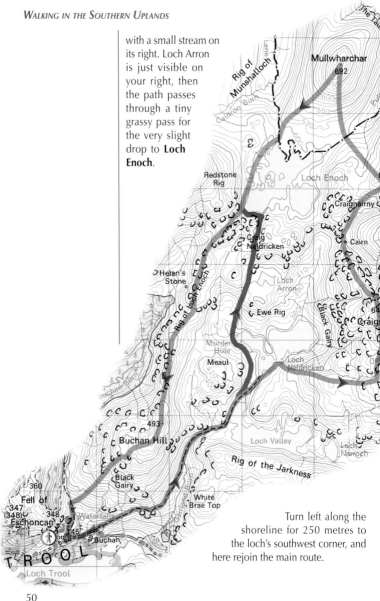

Turn left along the shoreline for 250 metres to the loch's southwest corner, and here rejoin the main route.

50

For the main route over the Dungeon Hills, at the corner of Loch Valley look out for the smaller path on the right, which runs up to the left of the Mid Burn. Cross the stream, then follow it up to the outflow of **Loch Neldricken**.

A very small wet path follows the loch's southern shore. After 500 metres, opposite a long promontory from the northern shore, turn uphill. Follow a broad spur-line up east onto the ridge of Craignaw. Along the broad crest the going is rather good, with slabs of bare granite leading up to **Craignaw** summit cairn.

The way off Craignaw is a little awkward even in clear weather. The best way down is to head just west of north (effectively, due north magnetic) over a small rise to find the top of a steep grassy valley. Head down this (still north) for 150 metres until below a band of rocks. Now contour left, with a slight rise onto a flat-topped spur. Here is the boulder-sprinkled slab called the Devil's Bowling Green. Follow the spur's flat top northwest, until a small path leads north down off its end to the col at Wolf Slock. ▶

Wolf Slock is named 'Nick of the Dungeon' on Harvey's and OS Explorer maps.

Here, at a cairn, the faint path divides. Ahead up to Craignairny takes in a fine view of Loch Enoch, but simpler is to take the path slanting up to the right, northeast. After 800 metres it fades away on the complicated knolly plateau. Keep ahead, to the plateau's eastern corner, to find the cairned high point of **Dungeon Hill**.

Descend northwest, over complex ground; but even in mist Mullwarchar is a nice large target to aim for. Pass through the wide col northeast of Loch Enoch and take the grassy slopes of **Mullwarchar** to its top.

In the 1980s Mullwarchar was mooted as a storage point for high level **nuclear waste**, to be sealed for millions of years in holes drilled deep into its granite lump. Doing anything at all with nuclear waste is a sure-fire vote loser for any party, and the radioactive waste still sits in an evil heap at Sellafield in Cumbria for future generations to deal with.

Daw
Spout
Loch

*Merrick from the granite slabs of Mullwarchar*

Walkers on the 'Three lochs' short-cut, as well as those diverting from Walk 5, join at this point.

Descend southwest to cross the outflow of **Loch Enoch**. A small wet path leads along the loch's west shore, rising a little above it to arrive just above its southwest corner. ◄

A fence and wall run up from the loch corner in a grassy hollow. At the top of the hollow, head up onto the ridgeline on the left, **Rig of Loch Enoch**. A small path follows the crest of this southwest, all the way to **Buchan Hill**.

A small preliminary cairn is actually the 493m high point, with the main cairn 300 metres further on. The summit ridge bends right, southwest, to a final cairn.

Slant down southwest. The upper slope of Buchan Hill has low crags called **Black Gairy**. The southwest direction from the summit leads into a wide grassy gap, with a rough path continuing below.

Continue slanting southwest, towards Buchan Burn. After some very rough ground near the burn, it may be possible to cross the burn to a well-used path on the western bank, and this leads down to the car park. Alternatively, if the stream is in spate, head straight downhill towards Buchan house to rejoin the track there and head up right to the car park.

# WALK 7
## *Rhinns of the Kells*

| | |
|---|---|
| **Start/Finish** | Forrest Lodge (NX 552 863) |
| **Distance** | 29km (18 miles) |
| **Ascent** | 1300m (4400ft) |
| **Approx time** | 9½hrs |
| **Terrain** | Forest tracks; a small amount of rough, tussocky ground; hill ridges and small paths |
| **Max altitude** | Corserine, 814m |
| **Maps** | Landranger 77 (Dalmellington); Explorer 318 (Galloway N) |
| **Parking** | Arrive along Forrest Road and go over a stone bridge with 2 ton weight limit to a car park on the left |
| **Variant** | Direct to Corserine then following southern half of ridgeline – 17.5km (11 miles) with 950m (3100ft) of ascent (about 6¼hrs) |

The Rhinns of the Kells is the Southern Uplands' finest ridgeline. On the left it drops steep and craggy to the Glenkens; on the right it looks into the rugged Galloway heartland. And each of its four hills has its own character – narrow, stony Carlin's Cairn; huge, sprawling Corserine; the rocky ridgeline of Millfire; and the rough lump of Meikle Millyea.

The trouble with a line is that its two ends are rather far apart. Walkers with two cars can be clever and get onto the ridge's northern end from Green Well of Scotland. Otherwise, there's a bit of guddling about in the plantations to start with. This is the necessary price if Carlin's Cairn is to be included – perhaps the finest peak of the ridgeline. However, there is a more straightforward route from Forrest Lodge westwards through the trees that gives direct access to Corserine (see 'Variant', below).

Tracks at the car park are more complicated than marked on maps. Take the main track north, crossing another stone bridge with 2 ton weight limit, to the gateway to **Forrest Lodge**; a statue of a piper is ahead. Bear left here on a rougher track (signed for Nether Forrest and Forrest Lodge). ▶ Pass round to the left of the lodge.

This track is not marked on Landranger and is incorrectly marked on Explorer maps.

After 800 metres roughly northeast, reach a T-junction with a major track. Turn up left for 150 metres to another junction. Keep left, and after 300 metres follow the track round to the right at an open shed.

This wide, smooth timber track runs roughly northeast, then north under the minor crags of **Craigmaharb**, and then northwest. After a side-track on the left (signed 'Mykola Lysenko Road') the main track swings north. ◄ It passes the crumbling shepherd's house **Darnaw** in woods to the left, and then bends northwest. There's a minor side-track on the right, and in another 250 metres the track bends left again. Go on for just 170 metres to turn right down a forest ride just west of north to **Polmaddy Burn**.

*Mykola Lysenko was a Ukranian musician.*

Cross the burn and head to the corner of the open ground around the former **Shiel of Castlemaddy bothy**. ◄ Pass through a broken wall to the masonry cairn commemorating the bothy demolition. A grassed-over track runs west, then uphill beside a wall and stream (it's blocked by fallen timber in places) to a forest track. Turn right for 300 metres, then go back sharp left. The forest track runs north through a col west of **Craigenwallie**, then downhill roughly northeast.

*Little used, sometimes abused, and becoming unsafe, the bothy was demolished in 2011.*

After 1km downhill, the track levels and bends right (east). Turn down left, between clear-fell (right) and mature trees soon for felling (left), to **Halfmark Burn**. Turn briefly downstream to crossbelow the Cleugh of Alraith (small gorge), and turn back upstream on a rough quad-bike track for 300 metres to the head of the cleugh, with a small waterfall.

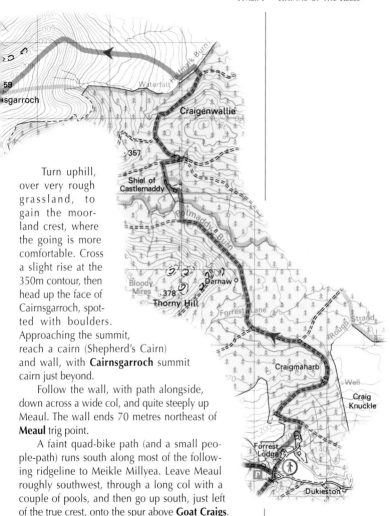

Turn uphill, over very rough grassland, to gain the moorland crest, where the going is more comfortable. Cross a slight rise at the 350m contour, then head up the face of Cairnsgarroch, spotted with boulders. Approaching the summit, reach a cairn (Shepherd's Cairn) and wall, with **Cairnsgarroch** summit cairn just beyond.

Follow the wall, with path alongside, down across a wide col, and quite steeply up Meaul. The wall ends 70 metres northeast of **Meaul** trig point.

A faint quad-bike path (and a small people-path) runs south along most of the following ridgeline to Meikle Millyea. Leave Meaul roughly southwest, through a long col with a couple of pools, and then go up south, just left of the true crest, onto the spur above **Goat Craigs**. The well-defined stony ridgeline runs southwest, then south with drops to the left, to the large and ancient cairn on **Carlin's Cairn**.

map continues on page 56

55

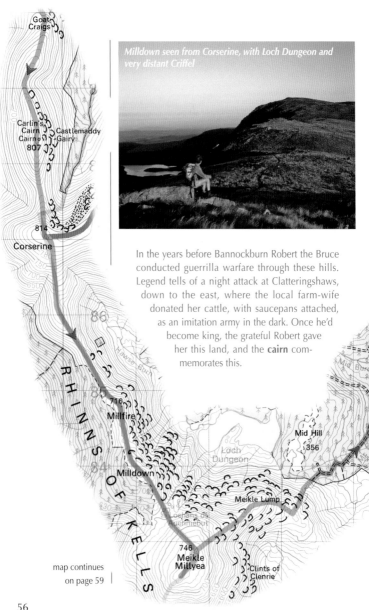

Goat
Craigs

Carlin's
Cairn
Cairn
807

Castlemaddy
Gairy

814

Corserine

*Milldown seen from Corserine, with Loch Dungeon and very distant Criffel*

In the years before Bannockburn Robert the Bruce conducted guerrilla warfare through these hills. Legend tells of a night attack at Clatteringshaws, down to the east, where the local farm-wife donated her cattle, with saucepans attached, as an imitation army in the dark. Once he'd become king, the grateful Robert gave her this land, and the **cairn** commemorates this.

86

Hawse Burn

R H I N N S

716
Millfire

Mid Burn

Mid Hill
356

Loch
Dungeon

O F

Milldown

Meikle Lump

K E L L S

Lochans of
Auchniebut

746
Meikle
Millyea

Clints of
Clenrie

map continues
on page 59

Carlin Cairn's southern spur, a col, and a rise – all south – lead to the trig point on the plateau of **Corserine**. The variant route arrives here from the east.

The descent line slants slightly left (south-south-east), and unless Millfire is visible ahead you need a compass (or GPS) line here. At 700m level the ridgeline reforms, running south and then southeast, with plantations just below on the right. Keep close to drops on the left for the small path to the cairn on **Millfire**. The ridge runs level for 800 metres, then rises; above the col a wall crosses, and now walkers have a guiding wall along the ridgeline. The summit cairn of **Milldown** is out to the left of the wall, above the steep drop to Loch Dungeon.

Wall and path run down through rugged ground to the small **Lochans of Auchniebut** for the final rise to **Meikle Millyea**. Arrive at a trig point and large ancient cairn. Harvey mapping has the true summit (749m) at the cairn 400

*On Millfire, looking back to Corserine*

metres southwest, and it's a pleasant plateau wander out and back to visit it (also gaining southward views to Loch Dee).

From the main cairn and trig point, turn downhill northeast, soon joining a broken wall with path alongside. The wall levels off along the shoulder **Meikle Lump**. ◄ The wall and path bend down east for 600 metres, then bend 90° left, to descend steeply northeast alongside a small stream.

Just above the forest fence, slant down left to a ladder stile into the trees. The ride ahead (blocked by a couple of fallen trees) leads in 200 metres to a forest track. Turn down right, ignoring a side-track left and passing an elevated wooden hide used for shooting roe deer. The track bends left (northeast) to a cross-roads. Keep ahead, on a wide, smooth track, with clear-fell to the left allowing views to Cairnsmore of Carsphairn.

Keep following the main track ahead and downhill. It passes between two houses at **Burnhead**, and joins Burnhead Burn to arrive at the car park.

### Variant – direct to Corserine

From the car park at **Forrest Lodge**, walk up the south bank of Polharrow Burn on 'Birger Natvig Road'. On the slope of Bennan Hill bear right, across the stream, which is the outflow from **Loch Harrow**. Continue uphill, northwest for 1km, for a rough path on the left into the trees.

It emerges onto the lower slopes of Corserine. Head quite steeply uphill, northwest, to the ridgeline near

*The summit, out to the left, has views across Loch Dungeon to Corserine.*

the shoulder **Craigrine**, and up southwest to the trig point on **Corserine**. Then follow the main route back to Forrest Lodge.

# WALK 8
*Cairnsmore of Carsphairn*

| | |
|---|---|
| **Start/Finish** | Moorbrock track end (NX 641 953) |
| **Distance** | 19km (12 miles) |
| **Ascent** | 1000m (3300ft) |
| **Approx time** | 7hrs |
| **Terrain** | Tracks; pathless grassy slopes and rounded ridges |
| **Max altitude** | Cairnsmore of Carsphairn, 797m |
| **Maps** | Landranger 77 (Dalmellington); Explorer 328 (Sanquhar) |
| **Parking** | Moorbrock track end 600 metres past Craigengillan; also limited verge parking at Craigengillan |

Cairnsmore of Carsphairn is climbed (when it's climbed at all) merely because of its being over 2500ft high. In such 'let's get it over with' mode, it's an up-and-down from Green Well of Scotland by the track and the ruined wall, with a descent over Dunool.

This walk comes at it from the back, giving a full day of Southern Upland strolling on pathless grass with not even a fence line to steer your feet. It shows walkers the slightly craggy eastern side, and leads across slopes peppered with granite boulders like cast-offs from a sculpture park. There is a lunch-stop in the handy Clennoch bothy.

Take the gated track on the left, signed 'Moorbrock Estate'. It rises across the foot of a hill spur, then leaves the trees with views to Moorbrock Hill and same-named farm at its foot. Keep ahead across **Polifferie Burn** and up to the farm.

The track passes above **Moorbrock farm** and drops to a small ford. Across this, turn left on the track up Moorbrock Hill beside **Poltie Burn**. The track bends left along the top of the trees, working gently up around the flank of **Green Hill** into the narrow valley entrance to the 'sanctuary' at the back of Cairnsmore.

A cluster of rounded **erratic boulders** of the Cairnsmore granite has been dropped off here by a small glacier. The bedrock at this point is the layered, deep-ocean greywacke rock, seen in the cutting alongside the track.

*Cairnsmore of Carsphairn seen from Beninner*

As the track heads upvalley above Poldores Burn, look out for a grassed-over old track forking up to the right. ▶ Follow this up northeast right onto the Moorbrock Hill plateau. Keep to the plateau's right-hand (east) side, along the top of the Moorbrock Gairy crags, to the small cairn on **Moorbrock Hill**.

Head northwest to the small sub-summit. Now quad-bike

This track was built for mineral explorations in the 1980s, then abandoned.

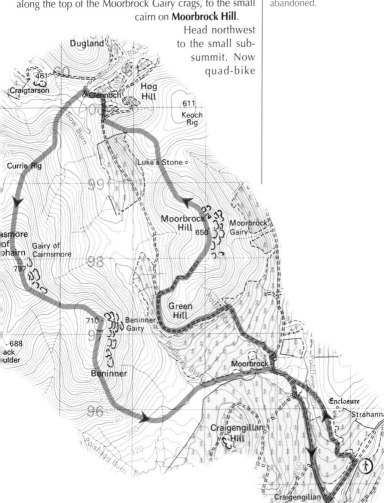

*Currie Rig of Cairnsmore of Carsphairn, looking towards Windy Standard windfarm*

wheelmarks lead down north and up to the moorland levelling called 'Alwhat' on the Explorer map. (Don't tick this on your 'Donalds' list, as it isn't the 626m Alwhat 4km northeast.) Head down a vague spur northwest, keeping to the right of a block of trees, to a track junction above the valley floor. ◀

This track, followed to the left, runs south to rejoin the outward route below Green Hill.

Take the lower track upvalley. It drops to cross a stream, rises past a junction, and drops again to **Clennoch bothy**.

> The east side of the valley is dominated by the **windfarm** on appropriately named Windy Standard. Built in 1996 this has historic status as one of the first in the Southern Uplands and indeed the UK. It is considered 'unintrusive' as not visible from roads and villages, although obvious enough to hillwalkers.

From the bothy cross the very rough valley floor, keeping to the right (north) of an area planted with birches and other broadleaf trees, to cross the **Bow Burn**. Cross a fence and head straight up the slope of Cairnsmore, weaving among the small granite outcrops of Craighorn. Pass a couple of shepherd's cairns to the grassy shoulder of **Currie Rig**, with pleasant, easy going to the trig point and large cairn on **Cairnsmore of Carsphairn**.

Leave the summit just east of south, keeping away from the steep drops of Gairy of Cairnsmore on your left. A fence arrives from the right. Cross a stile at its corner, and go down the boulder-peppered slope to the right of the fence to the col Nick of the Lochans. ▶ Here there's a stile across a side-fence. Go straight up the grassy slope to the cairn on **Beninner**.

Again there's a 'gairy', a craggy east-facing slope, to work around before you can descend to Moorbrock. Leave Beninner summit just west of south until the slope starts to steepen, then drop southeast. Keep to the right for less steep ground.

At the slope foot head across moorland, aiming towards the stream and tree gap that leads towards the white farmhouse. Cross the first moorland east and cross a south-flowing stream, then turn left on a faint quad-bike path just beyond. This leads northeast to **Poldores Burn**. Follow the stream banks down through a wide tree gap. Near Moorbrock, where the stream bends down to the right, keep ahead to rejoin the farm's access track.

Turn down the track (retracing the outward route) for just 400 metres, then fork right on a long-abandoned old track for an alternative route down the valley. The grassed-over former track runs down to a crumbling stone bridge to join a forestry track. Turn left on this, following the Polifferie Burn out to **Craigengillan**, and turn left to return to the walk start.

The lochans are only a few metres across, and dry up in high summer.

# WALK 9
## Screel Hill

| | |
|---|---|
| **Start/Finish** | Screel Hill car park (NX 800 546) |
| **Distance** | 8km (5 miles) |
| **Ascent** | 550m (1600ft) |
| **Approx time** | 3hrs |
| **Terrain** | Tracks, paths; rough over Bengairn |
| **Max altitude** | Bengairn, 391m |
| **Maps** | Landranger 84 (Dumfries); Explorer 312 (Kirkcudbright) |
| **Parking** | Forestry Commission car park just up the Gelston side road off A711 |
| **Variant** | Omit Bengairn – 5km (3 miles) with 350m (1100ft) of ascent (about 2hrs) |

Ben Sgritheall is a tall, tough hill above Loch Hourn in the Western Highlands. This Screel, in the Stewartry of Kirkcudbright, is pronounced the same and means the same – Scree Hill. It has the same superb sea view and a similarly rocky top. However, this top is much more conveniently situated, just 343m above the sparkling water of Solway. At only a morning's walking, you'll not make a meal of Screel, but it's a superb little snack – a 200 calorie crunchy bar for the feet. For afters, we bite off the slightly bigger Bengairn.

Follow the forest track up out of the **car park** (or, 20 metres before the vehicle barrier, shortcut directly uphill on a well-marked path – the left hand of two up out of the parking area – to join the track above its first bend). The track bends back right, then turns uphill to a T-junction. Cross into the path directly ahead. It runs up through a young wood of birch and oak.

The path crosses another track at a bench and continues ahead up under mature needletrees – the path isn't always clear on the pine needles. It passes through a wall gap and continues directly uphill. It emerges from trees at the foot of Screel's heathery southeast spur.

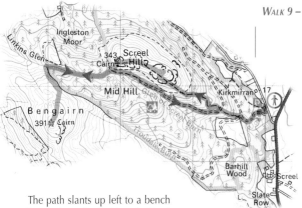

The path slants up left to a bench
on the southern flank. Here it dips for
20 metres. ▶ The main path slants up the
southern flank, below small crags, then turns abruptly
uphill and back to the right before following a final rocky
few steps to Screel's south summit, with the sea views.

On the right now
is a smaller, more
direct path to Screel's
south summit.

Bengairn is the western outlier of the Criffel granite.
Alongside it, the surrounding greywacke has been
baked and hardened by the granite magma into

*From Bengairn
summit to
Auchencairn Bay*

a blocky, sharp-edged rock called **hornfels**. This tough hornfelsed greywacke forms the upstanding ridge of Screel Hill.

Turn along the 1km of summit ridge, the path mostly peaty with rocky lumps, to the large cairn on the main top of **Screel** at its western end. The path descends, somewhat eroded, off the steep hill end.

At the foot of the steep descent, a path turns off left. ◄ But continue ahead, with clear-fell to the left and a wall and mature trees to the right. The faint path rises slightly, west, through a soggy col, then descends alongside the forming **Linkins Burn**. At the end of the clear-fell, cross a wall and turn up left alongside the edge of the clear-fell. After 200 metres, follow the wall up to the right away from the clear-fell. After another 200 metres uphill the wall levels off. Here cross it for a path slanting to the right to the trig point and cairn on top of **Bengairn**. ◄

Return to the corner of the clear-fell at Linkins Burn and head back through the soggy col. ◄ At the base of Screel's steep rise, turn right on a small path through felled ground, passing through the small col and descending the little valley along the base of Screel. Keep to the left of **Glen of Screel Burn**. The path runs to the corner of a forest track. Follow this down ahead, with sea views. The track bends slightly left, and levels at the bench passed on the outward route.

Return down the peaty path to the car park.

Take this left-hand path for the variant return (omitting Bengairn) to the car park.

Rocks here are rounded grey granite.

The short-cut route continues from here on the small path east.

# 2 NITHSDALE AND LANARKSHIRE

*On Well Hill, looking to Lowther Hill (Walk 13)*

# INTRODUCTION

Nithsdale forms the inland edge of Galloway, running right through the hill mass from the Solway to Ayrshire. Here starts what could be called the default Southern Uplands – rounded grassy hills, with easy going offered by shepherds' quad-bike tracks and guiding fence lines.

Old boundary it may be, but today the hills on both sides of the Nith are all in Dumfriesshire. The local lord, at Drumlanrig Castle, is Buccleuch and Queensberry, who takes the second half of his title from the southernmost of these hills (Walk 12). His ancestors lie entombed at Durisdeer (Walk 13), and over the centuries they created the elegant parkland appearance of the glen.

The old county of Lanarkshire stretches from the Southern Uplands into the edge of Glasgow. Motorists can identify Lanarkshire by its reddish roads, coloured by stone chips from the felsite of Tinto Hill (Walk 15). Tinto itself, standing out into the Lowland plain, is complemented by the grassy wilderness of the Culter Fells (Walk 16) and by the small but stylish Broughton Heights (Walk 17).

## WALK 10

*Afton Water*

| | |
|---|---|
| **Start/Finish** | Afton Glen – track end of Blackcraig farm (NS 631 080) |
| **Distance** | 13km (8 miles) |
| **Ascent** | 700m (2300ft) |
| **Approx time** | 5hrs |
| **Terrain** | Rough tracks and pathless grass |
| **Max altitude** | Blackcraig Hill, 700m |
| **Maps** | Landranger 77 (Dalmellington); Explorer 328 (Sanquhar) |
| **Parking** | Pull-in on uphill side of the road 200 metres south of the start; verge parking further south |
| **Variant** | Via Ern Cleuch – same distance but slightly more scrambly |

Green braes, sweet-scented birks and a murmuring stream – while it was poetic exaggeration for Robert Burns to claim that 'daily he wandered' Afton's hills, they're certainly worth a visit. The poem is 'Afton Water', in the voice of a lovesick shepherd on Blackcraig Hill. At only 13km, this route offers beauty plus bleakness, with plenty of time for poetical musings along the way.

The Afton hills are green and easy, but with little craggy bits, as well as those murmuring rills and so on. The there's a drop to Craigbraneoch Hill where Robert the Bruce's guerrilla army dodged among the boulders, probably not taking time to enjoy the view across the whole of the Lowlands – on a crisp winter afternoon, snow-covered Ben Lomond may show itself beyond.

For 150 years singers of Scotland have been urging the sweet Afton to flow gently. Finally the South of Scotland Water Board did something about it, taming its waters into a big blue reservoir with a fine dam and accompanying earthworks. Cross the dam, then finish the day up what could be Scotland's shortest scramble.

The Blackcraig track is unsigned – as walkers arrive from New Cumnock, it starts immediately before the first cattle grid, where the valley road becomes unfenced. Follow it over Afton Water towards cream-coloured **Blackcraig farm**.

The track leads round to the left of all the buildings, through a gate with kissing gate alongside, and up to the left of a wood. At the wood top, another gate with a green waymark arrow leads onto open hill.

A plantation is up on the left, with wind turbines on Hare Hill rising behind. Carry on up the rough track, which lies over an older path.

### Variant – Ern Cleuch

'Ern' is probably a reference to the erne or sea-eagle, while 'cleuch' is a little ravine of scree and stones. You won't see the sea-eagle, but you can at least explore the ravine.

Where the track moves away from the stream on its right, at 430m, cross the stream and head up beside a side-stream, southeast, into the little ravine with water-fall. Escape to the left of the waterfall up a scree runnel onto open hill above. Head straight up southeast to join the ridgeline fence, and turn right alongside it towards Blackcraig summit.

The track becomes soggy for a while, then as the slope eases it passes two cairns to reach a gate at the **Quintin Knowe** ridgeline.

Don't go through the gate, but turn right alongside the fence. Where ground along the fence is marshy, it may be better to move out to the right. ◀ After 1km of gentle ascent, the ground becomes rather rocky. Keep south along the plateau, with the fence on your left. A fence crosses, with a stile at its highest point. In another 200 metres reach the trig point, and **Blackcraig Hill**'s small summit cairn 50 metres to the south.

The Ern Cleuch variant rejoins here.

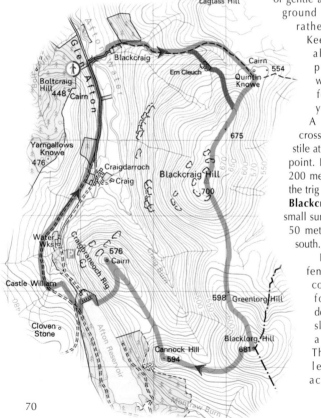

Rejoin the fence at its corner, and follow it down grassy slopes into a wide col. The fence leads on across the

## AFTON WATER

*Flow gently, sweet Afton! amang thy green braes,
Flow gently, I'll sing thee a song in thy praise;
My Mary's asleep by thy murmuring stream,
Flow gently, sweet Afton, disturb not her dream.
How lofty, sweet Afton, thy neighbouring hills,
Far mark'd with the courses of clear, winding rills;
There daily I wander as noon rises high,
My flocks and my Mary's sweet cot in my eye.*

The full text of Robert Burns' poem can be read at the Burns Cairn, erected by the local Burns club, on the Afton Water road 2km into the glen.

col. It climbs the far slope for 200 metres; where it bends away to the left keep straight uphill to the summit of **Blacklorg Hill**. ▶

Here three fences meet. A waymark points down right to follow a fence and broken wall down west. The fence bends left and back right for the short rise to **Cannock Hill**.

For more grassy tops, continue over Meikledodd, Alwhat, Alhang and Windy Standard, with a descent over Wedder Hill and Lamb Hill.

*On the way down Cannock Hill towards Craigbraneoch Hill*

71

*Scrambling on
Castle William*

After a fairly steep descent the fence turns down left; here keep ahead on a quad-bike path northwest towards the rocky top of Craigbraneoch Hill. Ignore a waymark pointing left, and continue to the fine little summit of **Craigbraneoch Hill**.

These craggy slopes are ideal for **guerrilla warfare**. Robert the Bruce's small army hid out here after his victory at Glentrool (Walks 5–6). The English couldn't catch him, despite the dog-napping of Bruce's own sleuth-hound to help them.

A frustrated Edward I came north in person, but died on the journey. His son Edward II occupied Cumnock Castle. By continuing to evade this less effective Edward, the wily Bruce (the Alex Salmond of the 14th century) started to make Scottish independence seem like a plausible cause – culminating at Bannockburn seven years later.

From Craigbraneoch head down steeply south, keeping to the left of any craggy ground. A strip of plantation masks the end of the **Afton Reservoir** dam – pass round its left corner for a path back along the reservoir shore to the dam end.

A track crosses the dam to a flagpole. Follow it to the left, alongside the reservoir, for 250 metres, to a junction.

Turn sharply back right on a higher track to the edge of the forest.

After about 100 metres, bear right off the track down to the rocky knob **Castle William**. It can be surmounted in style by a slab scramble on its uphill side or easily walked up. About 50 metres south is the small William's Pinnacle, a very short scramble of its own.

Slant back uphill to rejoin the track. It slants down to pass above two little plantations and join the valley road just north of **Craigdarroch farm**. The Blackcraig track end is 1km north along the road.

## WALK 11
### *Criffel*

| | |
|---|---|
| **Start/Finish** | New Abbey (NX 964 663) |
| **Distance** | 12km (7½ miles) |
| **Ascent** | 600m (2000ft) |
| **Approx time** | 4½hrs |
| **Terrain** | Rough paths that can be very wet |
| **Max altitude** | Criffel, 569m |
| **Maps** | Landranger 84 (Dumfries); Explorer 313 (Dumfries) |
| **Public transport** | Bus 372 (Dumfries–Dalbeattie) |
| **Parking** | Large car park at Sweetheart Abbey; also very limited parking at the Criffel lane end (NX 956 654) |
| **Variant** | Starting at Criffel lane end, the small car park under Waterloo Monument, gives 9.5km (6 miles) and same ascent – saving 45mins but missing some enjoyable, and fairly dry, valley paths. |

Standing alone on the Solway shore, Criffel has tremendous views north into the Southern Uplands, out to sea, and across to the English Lake District. And the sightline also works in reverse – Criffel is familiar to walkers on Skiddaw and Grasmoor, even though they may not all be able to name it.

The hill is a huge lump of granite, smeared with peat and heather. It's an atmospheric place, where warlord Douglas of Morton may (or more probably may not) lie buried under the summit cairn. The Norsemen named it Kraku-fjall, 'the Crow (or Raven) Hill'; Iron Age locals built an island refuge on Loch Kindar in Criffel's shadow.

However – heathery peat absorbs rainwater, and the granite doesn't form stream hollows to drain it away. Criffel is a soggy hill. For most of winter, or after heavy rainfall, or following the mid-March Criffel hill race, its paths degenerate into black peat-slop. You may prefer to tackle Screel (Route 9) instead and save Criffel for a dry spell.

Head into **New Abbey**, bearing left at the Abbey Arms to the mill pond. Here turn left, signed for Waterloo Monument. At once look for steps up left to a small path that shortcuts a bend in the lane. The enclosed path exits into a field; head up its left edge to rejoin the lane above.

*This is the start point for the slightly shortened version of the walk.*

Follow the lane for 800 metres, when it ends at a small car park. ◄ Bear left, signposted 'Criffel', over a track bridge.

The track continues alongside Glen Burn, passing to the right of **Mid Glen house**. Keep ahead on a path, which bends away from the stream and runs up under woodland, then plantations, to join a forest track.

*Douglas's cairn at Criffel summit*

Turn up this for 200 metres and round a bend to the left, then keep ahead on a waymarked path under the trees. It bends up to the right, heading up with a wall on its left. At the 250m contour it leaves the plantation through a broken wall. The path continues straight uphill, quite steeply but still boggy, to the cairn on **Knockendoch**.

The path dips slightly through the col behind Knockendoch, then runs up the left (east) flank of the rounded, heathery ridge towards Criffel. It runs up through some grassed-over peat hags, which offer sheltered lunch-spots. Then the ground levels to the big cairn and trig point at **Criffel** summit.

Return on the approach path for 200 metres, then fork right on a peaty path that descends rough grassy slopes towards Loch Kindar and the Nith Estuary. As the heather line is reached the path becomes a wide, wet band of trodden peat, but this goes on for only 400 metres to a gate at the top of the plantations. From here a very well-made path runs down to the right of Craigrockall Burn (ignore a footbridge on the left).

Trees in the stream strip are scrubby broadleaf, still allowing views ahead. The path crosses a forest track and descends to a second one low down on the hill, signposted to the left for New Abbey.

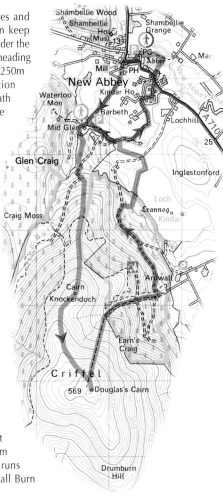

## CRIFFEL BOULDERS

With no towering precipices in the Southern Uplands, rock climbers have to be ingenious. The rounded granite boulders of Criffel provide bouldering sport on Airdrie Hill, 3km south of the summit. They're best reached from the forest roads to the southwest. The other spot for mini-mountaineering hereabouts is the Thirlstane, a pierced sea-stack southwest of Criffel (NX 991 565).

Meanwhile, one enterprising boulder has made it all the way down into England. The Erratic Boulder on Cannock Chase, Staffordshire, has been recognised as originating on Criffel, and so provides a clue to glacier flows during the Ice Age.

*This ground was clear-felled in 2014 so has views ahead over Nithsdale.*

The track runs gently downhill. ◀ At a junction after 600 metres a waymark indicates the track ahead. In 500 metres, as the track bends left, another waymark points right for a pleasant green path. This descends through woodland and runs above **Loch Kindar** to a kissing gate. Turn down right to a second gate into a loch-side field.

Follow the loch side round to the field's corner. Turn left along the field edge, crossing a farm track (signpost on the right) and then a small ditch bridge. A kissing gate is on the right just before the field's furthest corner.

Through the gate, a path runs between a ditch and a stone field wall to join another track, with a combination gate ahead (it opens either as wide farm gate or as small person gate).

### Return to Waterloo Monument car park

Walkers who started at the Waterloo Monument car park on the shorter version of the walk now turn back left along this track. Just through another combination gate, bear right on a grassier track, with trees to the left. Ignore a gate on the right, but as the track bends into the woodland take another combination gate ahead. Cross the long field ahead to a gate near the Waterloo Monument car park.

Go through the gate ahead on a track which crosses a stream and bends right. It runs between fields and through

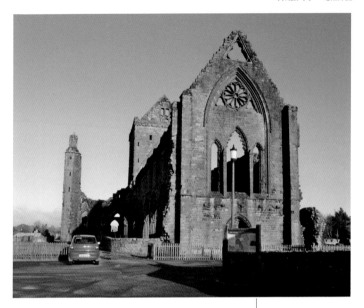

*Sweetheart Abbey*

a couple more gates to the edge of **New Abbey**. The track bends right, emerging between ornamental gateposts.

Take the street ahead, bending left to reach the **A710** at a duck pond. Turn left for 100 metres, past the primary school, then cross into a signed footpath. It runs past a playing field and becomes narrow and enclosed. After a kissing gate, turn left alongside the old granite boundary wall of Sweetheart Abbey.

> **Sweetheart Abbey** was built in 1273 by Lady Devorgilla of Galloway to commemorate her husband, John Balliol. His embalmed heart is buried within the abbey.

Steps lead up left to a gate into the abbey graveyard. A gate alongside the abbey leads out into its **car park**.

# WALK 12
## *Queensberry*

| | |
|---|---|
| **Start/Finish** | Mitchellslacks road end (NX 964 960) |
| **Distance** | 20km (12½ miles) |
| **Ascent** | 900m (3000ft) |
| **Approx time** | 7hrs |
| **Terrain** | Tracks; pathless grassy slopes and ridges, with some tussocky ground and one steep descent; 3km hill road to finish |
| **Max altitude** | Queensberry, 697m |
| **Maps** | Landranger 78 (Nithsdale); Explorers 321 (Nithsdale) and 329 (Lowther Hills) |
| **Parking** | Small parking area beside the green footpath signpost |
| **Variant** | Short-cut back from Earncraig Hill – 15km (9½ miles) with 700m (2300ft) of ascent (about 5hrs) |

The Lowthers rise out of the Dumfriesshire plain just 30km up the motorway from the English border. These are grassy, bleak hills, divided by charming valleys and cut with cleuchs – steep V-slots carved by streams and inhabited by wild goats.

Queensberry is the highest of the southern Lowthers, and also the closest to England. So it has, in crisp spring weather, outstanding views to Pennine, Lakeland, Solway and Galloway. The hill gave its name to the dukes of Queensberry. The second Queensberry duke was the man who dismantled the previous Scottish parliament in 1707. For his useful service he received a pension of £3000 and the dukedom of Dover. During these early days of the renewed Scottish parliament, Scots democrats may take particular pleasure in trampling all over Queensberry!

These rounded ridges allow fast progress, so the walk entails a fairly long day over the short grass. An early turn-back can be made from Earncraig Hill or from just before Gana Hill.

From the green footpath sign descend a quad track to join the driveway track below. Follow it left across **Capel Water**. At a track T-junction, another green sign points right for

Beattock by two routes, but turn left to pass **Mitchellslacks farm** (most buildings on your left). Beyond the farm the track becomes small and grassy. After the second gate, which leads onto open hill, bear right on the main track. It rises, then runs along above **Capel Burn** down left.

*Queensberry from Capel Water*

> Across the stream, opposite the Law, appears a level **shelf-line**, a 'parallel road' (a track runs along part of it). Note how some stream hollows descend to its level but do not continue below; they formed themselves when this shelf was the shoreline of a glacier-dammed lake.

A small knoll, **The Law,** rises above the track. In front of it turn back sharp right on a stony track that bends around the base of The Law. It makes a wide sweep to the left, then back right to sheep-handling pens.

Go through a gate and pass to the left of the sheep pens to cross the stream above. A quad track slants up to the right. Where it levels off, keep uphill to the cairn on the shoulder called **High Church**.

map continues
on page 82

Immediately southwest of the small summit a little **rocky channel** crosses the ridgeline, then turns downhill in a stony-sided dry gorge. It can't be a river valley as there's nowhere for a river to have flowed from... But that's just what it is – a 'meltwater channel' that formed when the empty space to west of the ridgeline was occupied by a glacier.

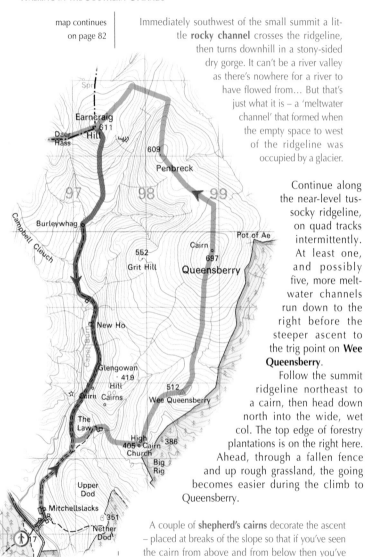

Continue along the near-level tussocky ridgeline, on quad tracks intermittently. At least one, and possibly five, more meltwater channels run down to the right before the steeper ascent to the trig point on **Wee Queensberry**.

Follow the summit ridgeline northeast to a cairn, then head down north into the wide, wet col. The top edge of forestry plantations is on the right here. Ahead, through a fallen fence and up rough grassland, the going becomes easier during the climb to Queensberry.

A couple of **shepherd's cairns** decorate the ascent – placed at breaks of the slope so that if you've seen the cairn from above and from below then you've

80

*Gana Hill and more distant Wedder Law from Queensberry summit*

covered the ground. Between them, a fircone-shaped cairn in a slight hollow appears to be a product of local artist Andy Goldsworthy, with stones added by less skilled later visitors (NX 98766 99271).

The grass gets shorter and slightly stony to the large sprawling cairn on **Queensberry**. The huge and ancient cairn is a place to linger on all but the nastiest of days.

Head down north to join a fence arriving from the right. In clear weather, keep to the left of peat hags in the col. In mist, it's easier to follow the fence through the right-hand edge of the hags. ▸

This fence appears on older Landranger maps as the former district boundary.

Grassy going northwest near the fence leads to **Penbreck**, where the fence turns north. Don't shortcut down left over steep scree ground, but keep down north with the fence. The final descent is rather steep, before walkers turn left with the fence across the head of the rather rocky Penbreck–Earncraig gap (Capel Yetts). Follow the fence up onto **Earncraig Hill**; it becomes a tumble-down wall across the summit.

At 2002ft (610m), **Earncraig Hill** used to be the lowest mountain in Southern Scotland – but the most recent survey has raised it by a metre, and Innerdownie of the Ochils takes on the 'least distinguished' distinction.

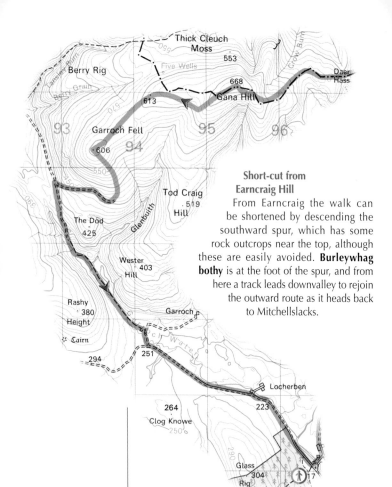

### Short-cut from Earncraig Hill

From Earncraig the walk can be shortened by descending the southward spur, which has some rock outcrops near the top, although these are easily avoided. **Burleywhag bothy** is at the foot of the spur, and from here a track leads downvalley to rejoin the outward route as it heads back to Mitchellslacks.

To shorten the walk take this track to the left, which runs back down south by Haggie Hill to Locherben. Then follow the road left to Mitchellslacks.

From Earncraig Hill head down steeply beside a fence and wall, among some very small outcrops, to cross **Daer Hass** col to a wall corner. Keep ahead onto a level knolly plateau, cross it west, and rejoin the fence, with a path alongside it up Gana Hill. At the shoulder (650m) a track joins from down on the left. ◄

Through the gate ahead, follow the track up to the summit of **Gana Hill**. A cairn on the right, beyond a fence, gives views over Daer Reservoir undisturbed by any track traffic.

Follow the fence along the summit ridge, with another cairn, to the left of the track, giving views over Nithsdale. The track wanders around a bit before running southwest along the flat ridgeline towards Garroch Fell. As the track bends down left, leave it and stroll up to **Garroch Fell** summit, where there's a large cairn and a wide view.

Slopes of heather and grass lead down southeast, soon with the track on your left. Descend beside it, moving onto the track as vegetation gets more heathery. The track bends right, contours around the slope, then slants down to join a wider track. Turn back left on this as it descends into the narrow sheltered glen of the **Garroch Water**.

This little valley has a rough shooters' hut in tarred fibreboard (open at the time of writing), and then its grassy track fords the stream five times. It leads out to sheep enclosures near **Garroch farm**. Turn right, across Garroch Water, to the hill road just beyond.

Turn left for just over 3km of quiet road back to Mitchellslacks.

*Fording Garroch Water*

# WALK 13

*Well Hill, Durisdeer*

| | |
|---|---|
| **Start/Finish** | Durisdeer (NS 894 036) |
| **Distance** | 9.5km (6 miles) |
| **Ascent** | 650m (2100ft) |
| **Approx time** | 3½–4hrs |
| **Terrain** | Grassy hills, with a green track for descent |
| **Max altitude** | Well Hill, 606m |
| **Maps** | Landranger 78 (Nithsdale); Explorer 329 (Lowther Hills) |
| **Public transport** | Bus 102 (Edinburgh–Dumfries via Thornhill) stops at Durisdeermill on A702 |
| **Parking** | Durisdeer |

Biggest often isn't best in the Southern Uplands. Ballencleuch Law (689m), the local high point, is a sprawling grassy hump. But Well Hill and its outliers are folded between two steep-sided glens, sculpted with hidden hollows and decorated with a midget earthwork. Add to that a start point at Durisdeer, the prettiest and most interesting village in Dumfriesshire.

Start at the war memorial in front of the church in **Durisdeer.** Head up the lane to the right of the church. It ends at a gate with signpost 'Wald Path'.

> The old track signed the **Wald Path**, once the coach road to Edinburgh, is usually known as the Well Path, as it leads to the Well Pass. That's the pass alongside Well Hill, so named because of having a spring of water on it. But some local toponymer knows better it would seem…

Continue along the track beyond for 50 metres to a gate on the left signposted for Black Hill. Through the gate bear right and slant down to a footbridge over the small stream. A quad-bike path leads up ahead onto the

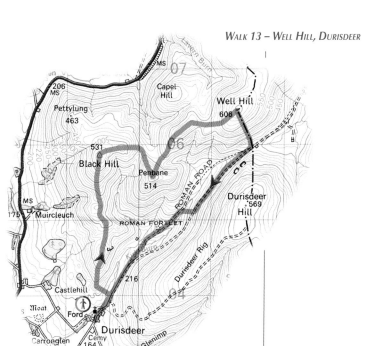

ridge of Black Hill. The path leads up the grassy slope
to a levelling, then down to a gate in a fence. The path
skirts left of the next ridge bump, but you could alternatively cross it then head left to rejoin the path near a
fence corner. The path heads up through a gateway gap
and zigzags up the upper steeper slope of the ridge to
**Black Hill** summit trig.

The quad-bike path bears down left towards
Pettylung, but keep ahead, leaving the summit northeast
then east. A fence is nearby on the left. Descend quite
steeply to join this fence at the col northwest of Penbane.

Walkers could now contour ahead across the base
of Penbane to the high point of the next col, but a fine
small summit is up ahead – so keep ahead up the spur of
heather and grass to the airy summit of **Penbane**.

*On the Well Path, looking down to Nithsdale*

Head down steeply north, dropping to the wide col Glenbo Hass. Cross the col and head up the slope to the long, narrow Turn Hill (529m), crossing the slant-wise fence near the top. (Alternatively, the fence could be followed to outflank Turn Hill.) A quad-bike path leads along the summit; at its end turn down rightto rejoin the fence at its corner. Follow it up to **Well Hill** summit.

Turn right through a gate and descend steeply with fence and broken wall (Lanarkshire boundary) on your right. The upper part of the wall is made not of greywacke but of crystalline quartz/feldspar from some intrusion or vein. The crystalline rock is iron stained, so probably a mineral vein. Pass through a gate to the Well Pass track (a hut, often unlocked, is just to the left) and turn right through the gate at the pass top. ◀

*For a 26.5km hill day, switch to follow Walk 14 here.*

Descend the smooth track for just over 1km. Ahead it leads down to Durisdeer, but below on the right a rough ladder stile crosses the valley-floor wall. Descend to cross this stile and the stream to a track just above. Turn down this to the Durisdeer **Roman fortlet**.

Continue down the track to a gate with signpost. The track fords the stream just beyond (there's a footbridge

## ROMAN LOWTHERS

The Romans didn't stop at Hadrian's Wall. For 300 years they controlled Britain as far as the Forth and Clyde. Their road north ran up the west side of the valley, and is still visible as a tractor track. The much better track on the east side is the 17th-century coach road (and is still a right of way for wheeled vehicles).

The small square earthwork above the Roman road is the best-preserved Roman fortlet in Scotland. It would have been topped off with a wooden palisade.

100 metres downstream if needed) then runs downvalley to rejoin the main Well Path track. Keep ahead down to Durisdeer, and turn right through an iron gate into the churchyard with its 17th-century sandstone graves. Behind the church, under a Russian-style dome, is the Queensberry tomb (sometimes locked). At the front of the church is a covenanter's gravestone.

If the **Queensberry tomb** is open it should not be missed. The second Duke of Queensberry helped engineer the dissolution of Scotland's parliament in 1707, and was rewarded by Queen Anne with a handsome pension. Part of it was spent on this high-concept marble monument with all the trimmings. The outdoor gravestones, in weathered red sandstone, are also worth a look.

# WALK 14
## Lowther Hill by Well and Enterkin passes

| | |
|---|---|
| Start/Finish | Durisdeer (NS 894 036) |
| Distance | 24km (15 miles) |
| Ascent | 850m (2900ft) |
| Approx time | 8hrs |
| Terrain | Old tracks and paths, linked by SU Way |
| Max altitude | Lowther Hill, 725m |
| Maps | Landranger 78 (Nithsdale); Explorer 329 (Lowther Hills) |
| Public transport | Bus 102 (Edinburgh–Dumfries via Thornhill) stops at Durisdeermill on A702 |
| Parking | Durisdeer |
| Variants | Start over Black Hill and Well Hill (Walk 13) – 26.5km (16½ miles) with 1100m (3600ft) of ascent (about 9hrs); take in East Mount Lowther (add 80m ascent and ¼hr) |

The upstart Southern Upland Way is just 30 years old, so check out two other paths that are older and even better. The Well Path's old coach road starts the walk, and on the descent Enterkin Pass is a green way through a deep hollow of the hills. Bonnie Prince Charlie came up here on his way north to Culloden. Before him, the place was just right for an ambush to liberate one of the Covenanters, religious extremists of the 1680s.

The village of Durisdeer has a bucketful of history, from Roman to Norman to the year 1707. On the way in there's the field bump of a Norman motte (NS 886 037). The village church has a Covenanter grave, and also the over-the-top tomb of the second Duke of Queensberry – find him through a black door at the back. He was one of the rogues who sold out the Scottish parliament in 1707. The path out of the village follows the valley of the Roman road, and there's a small fort of theirs (NS 903 049 – see Walk 13).

Count in with this the puffball dome of today on Lowther Hill, and it all adds up to 24km and 2000 years of top Southern Upland.

The lane to the right of the church at **Durisdeer** becomes a track, signed as Wald Path. Keep on the main track, uphill to the right of the stream.

After 800 metres, there is a sign on the left for **Durisdeer Fortlet** – an interesting detour. After the fort, follow the track another 500 metres, cross the stile down right and head up to the main route.

At the head of the valley pass through a gate with old stone posts. ▸ The track runs past two iron shacks. As it dips to the flat valley of **Potrail Water**, the main track leads to the left of a felled plantation and up to a mobile phone mast on the **A702**.

If you started over Black Hill and Well Hill, you rejoin the route here.

For antiquarian interest, cross the road to a grassy groove in the moor, the line of the Roman road. ▸ This leads to a roadside quarry (parking area). A Southern Upland (SU) Way signpost is seen at the roadside below.

Alternatively, turn right along the road.

Along the SU Way, there are boxes called **kists** at various distinctive points. Each contains a trove of souvenir coins, or 'waymerks' – a merk being an old Scots coin worth six shillings and eight pence. One kist is to be found between here and Lowther Hill; another is on Walk 19.

map continues on page 91

Head uphill to the left of a plantation, then to the left of a wall, to a ladder stile. Across this, the SU Way follows wall and fence to the left (southwest) up **Laght Hill**. The path, to the right of a fence and wall, drops steeply into a gap, then heads up **Comb Head**. Path and fence follow its crest over a minor top, then a further slight rise to **Cold Moss**.

Another 300 metres after the summit, the way-marked path turns half-right, away from the fence, to

89

Southern Upland Way crosses Cold Moss on the way up Lowther Hill

In mist it's better to stay with the fence.

avoid a steep col ahead. ◄ The path drops northwards with a few waymarks, passes below (and right of) the col, and heads up the grassy slope of Lowther Hill, rejoining the fence below the Lowther Hill dome. The protective dome was blown away in a gale of 2013, leaving the radar exposed to view.

Here the SU Way shortcuts left over a stile, but head around the dome's enclosure to the right to reach the road arriving from Green Lowther. Turn left, and at the crossroads on **Lowther Hill** summit turn right to exit the enclosure. Turn left to a fence and go down it northwest past a metal box-shelter and a stile on the SU Way. Join a gravel track down onto the narrow neck of grass leading towards East Mount Lowther.

**Variant – via East Mount Lowther**
The Enterkin Pass, on the main route, is a dramatic path – and sheltered from the weather. Against that, East Mount Lowther is the most attractive 2000-footer of this group.

Keep ahead along the col and up the green track to the viewpoint indicator at **East Mount Lowther** summit.

It correctly identifies the Paps of Jura as being visible from here. It also suggests that the real name of the hill is Auchenlone. The 'East Mount Lowther' name is an oddity – of all the Lowthers, this one is the furthest to the west.

The fence ahead is not a useful guide; cross it and head south along the top of the steep drop towards **Enterkin Burn**. After 800 metres almost level, continue south down the spur alongside the Enterkin hollow. At its foot, keep left of a fence to meet a farm track. Turn down left to the ford and footbridge over Enterkin Burn

map continues on page 93

at the foot of the Enterkin Pass.

At the low point of the col before East Mount Lowther, turn left over a stile to take the small path running down the steep-sided **Enterkin Burn** valley. A low-voltage

## THE ENTERKIN RESCUE

Dr John Brown's account of the 1850s compares the Enterkin with the Pass of Glencoe – but admits that the comparison isn't exact, as Enterkin is a whole lot wilder and more exciting. While we may not share the author's enthusiasm, Enterkin does have its own bit of bloodstained history from eight years before the Glencoe Massacre.

In summer 1684, nine Covenanters were being led up the pass, tied to their horses, on their way to Edinburgh to be tortured, executed or transported to the plantations. A rescuing party, led by James ('Long Gun') and Thomas Harkness of Locherben (Walk 12), set an ambush in the steep-sided part of the pass. The place is known as Keltie's Linn, after the soldier who died here. Two of the prisoners were shot by the soldiers, while the rest escaped into the hills.

Soldiers from the Highlands were transferred to Galloway to subdue the country and try and track down the rescuers. They were led by a local laird, John Graham of Claverhouse, nicknamed 'Bluidy Clavers' for his cruelty against the Covenanters. After the change of regime to William of Orange, Graham led the same Highlanders in defence of the deposed Stewart king, James II, during the Jacobite rebellion. Graham's death at the battle of Killiecrankie transformed 'Bluidy Clavers' into 'Bonnie Dundee'. But the Jacobite rebellion fizzled out after the follow-up battle at Dunkeld (1689).

Some disgruntled MacDonalds returning from that battle called in on hereditary enemy Robert Campbell of Glenlyon, looted the place and stole his kitchen furnishings. Three years later, Glenlyon commanded the 120 Campbell soldiers billeted in Glen Coe to carry out the notorious massacre. So while Glen Coe and Enterkin do not correspond in their scenery, they are linked through the complex loyalties of 17th-century Scotland.

The variant over East Mount Lowther rejoins here.

power line accompanies the path. At the level valley floor below, the path crosses the stream several times, ending just above it on the left. At the valley end a track crosses, with a footbridge over the stream. ◄

Follow the track left, slanting uphill above the stream, through a gate. Where the track bends back left, take a smaller track ahead, and in 100 metres bear left through a gate onto a green path. It runs along the valley wall high above the stream, then after 500 metres eases up left to reach the ridgeline. Join the fenced hedge along the ridge crest (south), with the Enterkin Burn far down

Enterkin Pass foot, looking back towards Lowther Hill

on the right. In the following col is the start of a new green track. After 2km it reaches the start of a tarmac lane.

Turn back left into a plantation on a small soft track. It drops to a gate with a signpost to Durisdeermill. The track leads down through **Eastside farm** to the A702. Turn right along the verge to **Durisdeermill**. Turn left into a lane, marked as having a ford ahead. ▶ After 1km cross the ford (footbridge alongside) at the edge of Durisdeer.

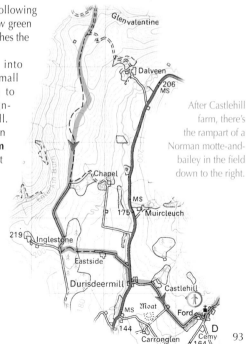

After Castlehill farm, there's the rampart of a Norman motte-and-bailey in the field down to the right.

# WALK 15
## *Tinto*

| | |
|---|---|
| **Start/Finish** | Greenhill Wood (NS 930 330) |
| **Distance** | 11km (6¾ miles) |
| **Ascent** | 500m (1700ft) |
| **Approx time** | 3½–4hrs |
| **Terrain** | Steep old path; grassy ridge; track and road |
| **Max altitude** | Tinto summit, 710m |
| **Maps** | Landranger 72 (Upper Clyde); Explorer 335 (Lanark) |
| **Parking** | Spacious pull-off at an abandoned plantation entrance |
| **Variant** | You could also start at Wiston, heading up the driveway of Wiston Lodge and keeping to the left of the lodge itself |

Technically, Tinto is a Lowland hill, standing 4km north of the Southern Upland boundary on the other side of the wide River Clyde. And when you get there, the pedants are correct. Tinto stands in splendid isolation, rising from flat lands that stretch northwards into the haze. And underfoot, instead of grey stones and heather, you're on grass and strange pink screes.

The popular path up Tinto is from the car park near Thankerton, returning the same way or with a slight variant over Totherin Hill summit. Here is a more satisfying circuit, steep up and gentle in the descent.

Follow the **B7055** eastwards, towards Wiston; after 1.5km fork left on the road signed for Wiston. After 1km, at the edge of **Wiston**, the road bends right and crosses the small West Burn. Here, just before a 'School' road sign, turn left on a path into the woods that lie around **Wiston Lodge**. In 20 metres turn left to a footbridge over the stream.

The path heads upstream, crossing and recrossing on footbridges, to the top of the wood. The path bends right, along the top of the woods, then continues with a kink right and left. At a reservoir building it joins the corner of a track. ◀ Turn left on a short path with a 'Tinto' waymark to a gate and stile at the corner of a field.

*If you started from Wiston you join the main route here.*

## PINK TINTO

The name 'Tinto' is probably not from the Spanish 'tinto', meaning coloured, but may be from the Gaelic 'teinnteach', meaning fiery red. The pink rocks are weathered to grey on Pap Craig, but are very striking on screes above and in broken walls. They are volcanic rhyolite lava, similar to the Pentland Hills (Walk 33). Some of them show sparkly mica crystals. Quarried for roadstone at Cairngryffe Hill 7km to the north, the Tinto red rock gives Lanarkshire roads a distinctive red surface, noticeable where you cross into the county.

On clear days, Tinto's views are outstanding – the summit topograph ambitiously includes Knocklayd in Ireland over 100 miles away. But on cloudy ones, there's another intriguing possibility:

> *On Tintock tap, there is a mist, And in that mist, there is a kist,*
> *And in that kist, there is a cup, And in that cup, there is a drap.*
> *Tak' up that cup, and drink that drap, that's in yon kist, on Tintock tap!*

Note that the rhyme doesn't specify what happens if you do drink it – a kist (wooden box) that appears only in hill fog has to be of faery origin.

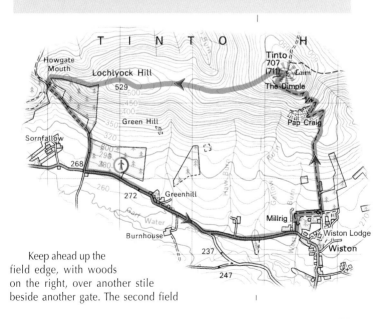

Keep ahead up the field edge, with woods on the right, over another stile beside another gate. The second field can be cow-trampled and muddy. Keep ahead up it – the path is arrow-straight, due north – and straight towards Tinto, towering ahead. At the field top take the left hand of two gates, with no stile, and continue uphill with a wall on the right. Cross a wide bench-stile and, as the wall turns away, a second bench-stile.

For a short way there is a fence is on the left, and then the path runs up the open hillside. It runs straight up towards Pap Craig, impending overhead in a way that's really rather mountainous. The path slants up to the right below the crags and scree to approach a fence on its right. Look out for the old path, in gentle grassy zigzags, rather than the more eroded modern variants that take the steep slope more directly.

The path zigzags up to the right of **Pap Craig**, then slants across left to the patch of flat ground above it.

A path heads up into the pink screes, slanting to the right to join two old fences and a fallen wall. A stile at the top leads up to the summit cairn on **Tinto**.

*Tinto's rocky shoulder, Pap Craig, seen from the path above Wiston Lodge*

The **cairn** is Bronze Age, possibly the largest on any Scottish hill, and rises at least 3m above the natural summit of the hill.

From the summit head westwards, which is towards 'Goatfell 60 miles'. Pass the trig pillar and head down alongside a fence and broken wall. After the first descent, the wall runs along a wide ridgeline, with a grass path beside it, and over the uncairned summit of **Lochlyoch Hill**. ▶

*'Lochlyoch' is misspelt as 'Lochlyock' on Landranger maps.*

Continue down the wall side, soon with a plantation on your left. At the plantation's bottom corner, cross a stile on the left. Head straight downhill – don't slant away sideways as there are old quarries hereabouts. Down a short steep slope reach a track junction. Take the track down to the left, all the way to the B7055 road.

Turn left ('Wiston 2¼') for 400 metres to the walk start.

# WALK 16
## Culter Fells

| | |
|---|---|
| **Start/Finish** | Birthwood, Culter Water (NT 032 310) |
| **Distance** | 18.5km (11½ miles) |
| **Ascent** | 700m (2300ft) |
| **Approx time** | 6hrs |
| **Terrain** | Grassy ridges, with fences; short peaty area at King Bank Head; track and estate road to finish |
| **Max altitude** | Culter Fell, 748m |
| **Maps** | Landranger 72 (Upper Clyde); Explorer 336 (Biggar) |
| **Parking** | Small parking pull-in on the Coulter Reservoir road just before the cattle grid where it becomes a private road |
| **Variant** | Chapelgill Hill adds 2km (1½ miles) – about 30mins |

The Culter Fells are rolling grass, heather and peat, cut through by deep stream valleys that give the group its character. Above these glens and combes, peat-free ground is found on the higher summits, the more sharply defined ridges and the steeper side-slopes. This excludes the six lesser, flatter summits of the group – if you want to taste the soggy tussocks, there's an optional diversion to Chapelgill Hill.

Return along the road for 300 metres, past the Culter–Cowgill junction, and turn right up the main driveway towards **Culter Allers farm**. This bends left among farm buildings. Just before reaching the farmhouse itself, bear right through a gate onto a grassy farm track.

The track runs north through a mixed wood. Where it zigzags back right, keep ahead through a gate and advance onto a **hill fort** just ahead (with views belying its 290m altitude). Turn right (southeast) across the slight col to a field gate. Go up then left, around the top corner of a fence. Descend to the bottom right corner of the small field, and follow a decaying electric fence up the hollow of **Nisbet Burn**.

Step across the fence at
a broken fence post and follow the stream up to a valley junction, where another dead electric fence arrives
from the right. Follow this to the left (northeast) up the

99

grassy-floored Dry Score hollow. At its head, a stream-eroded stony scaur leads to a sudden arrival at the col above.

Turn right on a quad-bike track beside a fence that crosses **Scawdmans Hill**. On the descent, a greywacke lump left of the fence makes a good spot for sitting on. From the col below, head up beside the fence until the top of the heather, then slant out to the left over grass and bilberry to reach the col south of Cardon Hill. A path and fence lead up north to **Cardon Hill** summit.

Return along the fence (actually one and a half fences – one old one and one very old and decayed). A brief rise leads to a fence junction implausibly named Birnies Bowrock (on Explorer maps).

### Diversion to Chapelgill Hill

Collectors of Donalds (Southern Upland 2000-footers) will want to gather Chapelgill Hill. From Birnies Bowrock head down south, or a bit east of south, to find a fence crossing the slope. Cross this and turn left, possibly finding a path or quad-bike trail parallel with the fence along the peaty, tussocky ridgeline. The final rise to **Chapelgill**

*Cardon Hill and Chapelgill Hill seen from the north*

*The folded valley of Culter Water leads down to the Coulter Reservoir*

**Hill** is pleasantly grassy. Return along the fence line to a fence junction southwest of Birnies Bowrock.

From Birnies Bowrock follow a fence down southwest. ▶ After a brief rise this turns south. There are grassed-over peat hags at the low point of the fence, before grassier ground on the rise to the trig point on **Culter Fell**.

A grassy path follows the fence southwards, over the gentle rise of **Moss Law** and down to **Holm Nick**. Here follow a rough track running down to the right alongside the small stream that's the head of Culter Water.

The track runs along the north side of **Coulter Reservoir**, then descends through two gates and becomes a tarmac estate road. Follow it down the green, peaceful valley for 3km to the walk start.

The spur is 'Dun Knees' – often a problem for older walkers.

# WALK 17
*Broughton Heights*

| | |
|---|---|
| **Start/Finish** | Walkers' car park, Broughton Place (NT 119 374) |
| **Distance** | 14.5km (9 miles) |
| **Ascent** | 1100m (3800ft) |
| **Approx time** | 6hrs |
| **Terrain** | Grassy paths and tracks with some steep slopes |
| **Max altitude** | Pyked Stane Hill (Broughton Heights), 571m |
| **Maps** | Landranger 72 (Upper Clyde); Explorer 336 (Biggar) |
| **Parking** | Follow signs 'Walkers' Car Park' to the left of Broughton Place to a pull-in at the track end by Shepherds Cottage |

Scottish hill-walkers may be familiar with Broughton Brewery, which produces a pint that slips down a treat after a hard day on the hill. Contrariwise, the Broughton Heights walk up a treat before a serious evening of beer...

Treats come in pint packages. The Broughton Heights are close to Biggar, but otherwise count as Smaller. Rising to just 571m, they plunge down again in a steepish slope of heathery grass, form a narrow green valley, and straight away rise to another shapely little hill. Baggers of Marilyns – those hills, however low, with 150m of clear drop round them – will get three on this walk. This makes this small range three times as hilly as the Dartmoor National Park.

The start is at a small castle, Broughton Place – actually a handsome 20th-century house in the old style. The walking is on grassy paths among the heather. The brewery is at the south end of the village, but the walk is found at the northern end on the road towards Edinburgh.

Go through a gate on a track that continues as the wide green path of the John Buchan Way. Follow it for a few steps past Shepherds Cottage, then bear off left across tussocks to cross **Hollows Burn** and head uphill on grass along the line of an old turf wall (fail dyke). There's a small path at the top as the dyke line runs into heather. At

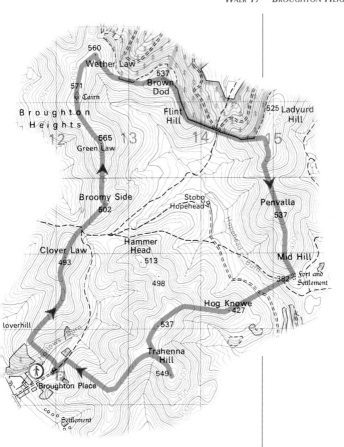

the ridge crest, turn right up a quad-bike path, with a wall nearby on the left.

Follow the ridge crest over Point 456m – the accompanying wall becomes a fence – and over **Clover Law**. Follow the fence down to the low pass, Cowiemuir Hass. ▶ Here there's a gate and stile on the path through the pass; cross the stile and continue ahead uphill to the left of the fence on a quad-bike path. From **Broomy Side**

Lakeland walkers will recognise the Norse 'hause' for pass.

*On the north ridge of Clover Law, with a view back to Broad Law and Culter Fell*

the fence leads north to **Green Law**. Now there are paths either side of the fence to the trig point on Pyked Stane Hill (marked as 'Broughton Heights' on Landranger).

Follow the fence north towards Wether Law. Just before the final slight rise, a quad-bike trail forks right, slanting down to the southeast ridge – or follow fences over the top of **Wether Law**. The descending southeast ridge joins a forest corner before its low point, after which the fence line rises to **Brown Dod**. Fork right, following the fence down to rejoin the forest edge, then rising gently to **Flint Hill**. Still alongside the forest, descend steeply (grassier slopes to the right) to the low col at the head of Gilshmuir Cleuch.

Take a gate on the left into the forest (there's a forest road bend just ahead). Continue ahead up the steep west spur of **Ladyurd Hill**, with easier going on the forest side of the fence. Explorer maps mark the 525m summit close to the fence corner. ◄

On Landranger, the 525m spot height is 400 metres away along the fence line to the north.

From the fence corner, follow two fences and a broken wall down south into a wide col. Keep ahead on a faint path straight up the face of **Penvalla**.

*On Ladyurd summit, heading to Penvalla*

A quad-bike path leads down just east of south onto the shoulder **Mid Hill**. As the slope eases, bear right over heather, past the cairn at the tip of Mid Hill and down south to a heather-covered **fort and settlement**. From the col just before this, head down to the right (west) in a grassy hollow, crossing the wide path that's the John Buchan Way and then the stream below. Head up south-west, crossing a track and slanting left to join a good quad-bike path up to the summit of **Hog Knowe**. The good path continues up the spur ahead to join a fence on Grey Yade (the north top of Trahenna).

Turn left alongside the fence, and in the following dip bear left on a path that slants down to the col northwest of Trahenna Hill. Go through a small gate and turn left, to the right of a fence, for 300 metres to **Trahenna** summit.

Return to the col and take a gate at the top of the side-fence ahead. Bear left on a small contouring path, continuing around to the fence descending the southwest spur towards Broughton. Follow this fence down to a slight col, where it bends slightly right. ▶ Keep slightly uphill alongside the fence for 100 metres to another

*A path bearing down right above the col descends Earn Cleuch to the John Buchan Way.*

105

*Broughton Heights at dawn, from the Pentland Hills*

slight bend right, and here turn downhill, right, on a quad-bike path.

The path descends the spur crest northwest. At the foot it keeps a little distance to the left of a plantation to reach the wide path of the John Buchan Way at the valley floor. Turn left to Shepherds Cottage.

# 3 MOFFATDALE

*Selcoth ravine and Croft Head from Ettrick Head (Walk 19)*

# INTRODUCTION

The long, deep Moffatdale leads through to the head of Yarrow Water to make a natural west–east through-route from Galloway and the Solway to the Tweed and Borders region. The quiet A708 follows it through from Moffat to Selkirk.

The hills on either side are the best of walking. Every one of them has some bonus feature that shows the Southern Uplands as more than merely big, green and grassy. Walk 18 has its devilish hidey-hole, the Devil's Beef Tub, and Walk 19 has the ravine below Ettrick Head. Hart Fell (Walk 20) offers the narrow arete of Saddle Yoke, while White Coomb (Walk 21) lies above the high tarn of Loch Skeen. Walks 23 and 24 rise above the twin valley lochs at Tibbie Shiels.

## WALK 18

*Devil's Beef Tub*

| | |
|---|---|
| **Start/Finish** | A701 above Devil's Beef Tub (NT 057 126) |
| **Distance** | 10km (6 miles) |
| **Ascent** | 550m (1800ft) |
| **Approx time** | 3½hrs |
| **Terrain** | Grassy paths |
| **Max altitude** | Chalk Rig Edge, 500m |
| **Maps** | Landranger 78 (Nithsdale); Explorer 330 (Moffat) |
| **Parking** | Small pull-in overlooking the Beef Tub; more parking 500 metres downvalley alongside monument viewpoint |

Why 'Beef Tub'? Looking from down Annandale, you wouldn't suspect that the smooth, simple curves of the glen had a hidden northwest corner and a scooped-out stony hole. So this made an ideal spot to hide away your cows when the Maxwells came raiding from the Nith, or the Armstrongs from the east, or the Grahams up out of England. And it's just as good a hiding place when it's you that's done the raiding, and the Armstrongs are looking to get their own cattle back…

And the Devil? Seen from the information board at the start of the walk, the huge rocky hollow has quite clearly been dug out by a Satanic spade – well, either that or a small corrie glacier from the Loch Lomond re-advance of 10,000 years ago.

The walk follows a loop at the top of the Annandale Way that forms a ready-made circular route around the Beef Tub, taking in what will one day be the reconstituted wildwood of Tweed Hope and is currently a forest of green plastic tree tubes. From Corehead it follows another and more exciting old pass to Tweeddale that leads right up through the Beef Tub to revisit its rim, perhaps in the lovely evening light.

Walk up the A701 to a forest gateway on the right. Take the wide gravel track for 100 metres, then bear right through a small gate signposted as Annandale Way. The path leads up, to the right of the plantation fence, to the trig point on **Annanhead Hill**.

The grassy path continues along the slope of Peat Knowe, with the wall and fence to your left and the hollow of the **Devil's Beef Tub** dropping to the right. The path drops gently to the head of a rocky little valley that drops into the Beef Tub. ▶ Here it meets the wall. Once around

Note the 'Strait Step' path contouring in across the steep face of Great Hill – this is your return route.

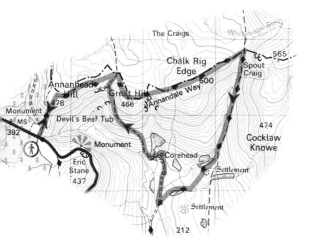

109

*Looking down into the Devil's Beef Tub from Peat Knowe*

the little valley head, bear right, away from the wall, straight up **Great Hill**.

The path leads down east, rejoining the fence and broken wall at a col with a waymark post. Keep ahead up to the right of the fence and along **Chalk Rig Edge**, then down to a rather soggy col at the head of Tweed Hope. Northwards, this little morass drains into the great basin of the Tweed; southwards, it is a source of the Annan, and is marked by a large cairn of the Annandale Way.

Turn right at the cairn, down a waymarked grass path that for 2km crosses the slopes up left from the Tweedhope Burn.

In the future **Tweed Hope** should become a birchwood, with hazel, oak, broom, juniper and other species. The Borders Forest Trust bought Corehead farm in 2009 and has planted 130,000 native trees as part of its plan to restore ancient ecosystems.

110

At the foot of the Tweed Hope valley the path reaches a gateway with an Annandale Way signpost. Here turn right and continue to a gate to the left of plantations above Tweedhope Burn's small gorge. Through this gate, bear left (waymark arrow), slanting down a field to a gate at its foot.

Through this gate keep ahead to the right of a tall deer fence, crossing a tiny stream and passing along to the right of a strip of trees. At their end, bear slightly left (southwest), passing through a final gate and joining the tarmac Corehead access track just north of its bridge over Tweedhope Burn.

Turn right, away from the bridge, to **Corehead farm**. Just before the buildings bear right at a signpost. Pass along a field foot to another signpost and gate, and here turn left behind the farm buildings. Cross a tiny footbridge and bear left to the bottom of a plantation. Keep ahead to a signpost at the plantation corner. ▸

The path line marked on local information boards is inaccurate here.

Turn uphill alongside the plantation to a fence. Turn left to a gate onto the open hill and keep ahead, slanting up around the slope of Great Hill, passing a tall signpost. The old path is now grassed over and quite faint on the ground. High on the side of Great Hill, the path passes a tiny stream trickle, with its peaty spring 10 metres up the slope beside a broken old cairn. This cairn is the Martyr's Stone (NT 0668 1297).

## THE MARTYR'S STONE AND MACLERAN'S LOUP

The stone commemorates John Hunter, a Covenanter shot by Colonel James Douglas in 1685 while escaping from Corehead house up this path towards Strait Step, where the dragoons could not have followed. Conveniently close to the mutual corner of Dumfriesshire, Lanarkshire and Peeblesshire (on A701 1km north of the walk start), the Beef Tub area was used for conventicles and Corehead was a known refuge.

*All who would not with their idols bow*
*They sought them out and whom they found they slew*
*For owning of Christs cause I then did die*
*My blood for veangeance on His en'mies did cry.*

A modern monument to John Hunter is placed more conveniently beside the A701 directly opposite.

'Macleran's Loup' (Macleran's leap) was probably taken from the Strait Step (rather than the A701), the leap to safety of a captured Jacobite soldier on his way to the gallows at Carlisle, who escaped by a sudden dash down into the Beef Tub. Witness to a more modern escape is a white van that lay for many years in the Beef Tub after an icy slide all the way down from the main road.

In another 200 metres the path levels off at Great Hill's vague southwest spur. ◀ Known as the Strait Step (meaning 'narrow path') it contours across a steep, rocky slope above the Beef Tub – at one point there's a rocky step across a little stream gully.

The path contours in along the side of the rocky little valley and rejoins the outward route at its head. Turn left on the path over Annanhead Hill to the A701.

If the path has been lost, perhaps in mist, head straight up northeast to Great Hill summit, keeping to the right of the steepest slopes.

*Strait Step path, high above the Devil's Beef Tub*

# WALK 19

*Ettrick Head*

| | |
|---|---|
| **Start/Finish** | Selcoth, Moffatdale (NT 138 078) |
| **Distance** | 19km (11½ miles) |
| **Ascent** | 1000m (3300ft) |
| **Approx time** | 7hrs |
| **Terrain** | Grassy hillsides, tussocky in a couple of places; some good paths |
| **Max altitude** | Loch Fell, 688m |
| **Maps** | Landrangers 78 (Nithsdale) and 79 (Hawick); Explorer 330 (Moffat) |
| **Parking** | Anglers' and walkers' car park near Selcoth fish farm |
| **Variant** | Omit Loch Fell – 16km (10 miles) with 850m (2800ft) of ascent (about 6hrs) |

It's argued that true mountain scenery has to be glacier scenery. However, the head of Ettrick shows just what can be achieved with streams. Croft Head is deeply carved on two sides, and the upper Selcoth Burn, leading to Ettrick Head, is a shaly ravine with the Southern Upland Way path balancing across the steep grass slope above.

Loch Fell, the highest of the group, is a more usual flat-topped, fence-guided Southern Upland. While it does offer new views south to Criffel and the Solway, the peak can be bypassed via a short-cut along the Southern Upland Way's most exciting mile. The ridgeline northwards from Capel Fell offers easy going, a couple more Donalds, and views the other way to Hart Fell and White Coomb.

Follow the smooth track past the fish farm to **Selcoth**. Keep ahead, below the buildings, and take the lower track to pass below a final bungalow onto open hillside. The track slants uphill for 600 metres, then bends back to the left to reach a gateway onto open hill.

In summer this slope has bracken and nettles, so follow the faint track uphill to the top of the nasty vegetation

*Heading down the northeast ridge of Croft Head*

zone, then strike up left onto the ridge crest. Follow it all the way up, joining a fence for the last few metres to **Croft Head** summit.

An unexpected SU Way marker indicates a high-level variant route developed for when the plantations below are being operated on. Follow the waymarks and small path down just north of east, initially with the fence on your left, towards the scoured-out hollow of **Selcoth Burn**. At the ridge end, the path carves into the hillside in zig-zags that lead down to a sheepfold at the head of the south-flowing Wamphray Burn.

## CRAIGMICHEN SCAR

As he did at the better known Dobb's Linn (Walk 21), the early geologist Charles Lapworth unravelled Craigmichen Scar's shale layers within the tougher greywacke rocks to make sense of the faulted and folded Southern Uplands. ('Scars' or 'scaurs' are eroded-out areas of scree and stones.) The flaky shale layers represent sea-bottom mud during long periods of nothing-much-happening. As such, they contain the graptolite fossils used by Lapworth as time markers within the rocks. The shale is seen and walked over on the short-cut route's stretch of the SU Way below Ettrick Head. Graptolites look like the marks of small threaded screws, typically 1mm wide and a couple of centimetres long; but the author's brief search didn't discover any.

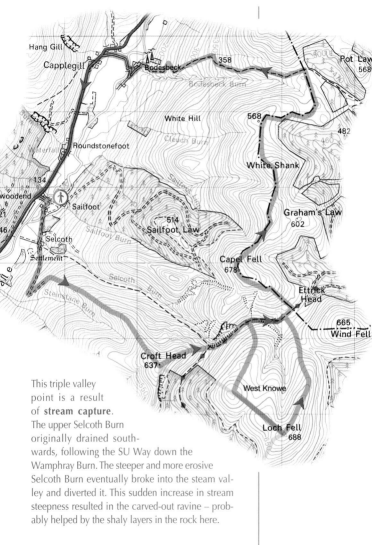

This triple valley point is a result of **stream capture**. The upper Selcoth Burn originally drained south-wards, following the SU Way down the Wamphray Burn. The steeper and more erosive Selcoth Burn eventually broke into the steam val-ley and diverted it. This sudden increase in stream steepness resulted in the carved-out ravine – prob-ably helped by the shaly layers in the rock here.

It is possible here to make a direct attack on the very steep slope of West Knowe, but it's better to follow the SU Way to the left above the Selcoth ravine to its highest point.

### Short-cut omitting Loch Fell

There's a small sculpture just above the path here.

Above Selcoth ravine, keep on along the SU Way as it dips to cross a charming footbridge. ◄ The path works its way up the slope above the stream to emerge at the gap of Ettrick Head. Follow it forward to the gate at the regional boundary, and here turn up left, with a green quad-bike trail to the left of the uphill fence.

Continue slanting uphill across the hillside to turn up the less steep ground of West Knowe's northeast spur. Pass a small stonefield and cross a flat plateau to the fence crossing **West Knowe**; the true summit lies somewhere behind the fence.

Follow the fence southeast, over the slight rise of East Knowe, to the trig point on **Loch Fell**.

Another fence leads down northeast. As the spur-line bends down north, slant away from the fence to follow the wide rounded crest. At its foot cross a boggy stream,

*Southern Upland Way above Selcoth Burn, with Croft Head behind*

and the SU Way just above, and head up the grassy ridge of Capel Fell, joining the fence on your right. ▶

The short-cut rejoins here.

The path and fence lead to **Capel Fell** summit, marked by a single broken fence post.

Follow the fence round a corner just beyond the summit and down northeast to a col. Go through a gate and continue alongside a wall over Smidhope Hill and **White Shank**. (White Shank's summit is to the right of the wall, which has plenty of broken gaps in it.)

The wall is falling into disrepair and has a fence beside it as it drops northwards then bends down to the right towards the forested Ettrick valley. The going beside the wall is rough and tussocky. The wall bends back north, following the ill-defined crest. At its lowest point a track arrives from the right and continues through a gate on the left as a rough tractor track.

This track slants down grassy slopes above (and to the right of) **Bodesbeck Burn**. After a gateway at the top of farmland, the track crosses a small stream. On this grass-land the track is indistinct, but it's just to the right of the small stream that runs down to join Bodesbeck Burn. The track, now clear, swings to the right and back again.

This track wiggle could just be to grant privacy to a **brownies' cave** – it's marked on the Explorer map in the gorge of Bodesbeck Burn below (NT 15432 09450). Behind summer foliage the cave wasn't vis-ible – perhaps the brownies object to the author's use of GPS for this purpose! There is also a little waterfall, if you can get in to see it.

At **Bodesbeck**, follow the driveway out to the left, then double sharply back right to a bridge over Moffat Water. Follow it out to the A708, and follow this quiet road left to Selcoth track end.

# WALK 20
*Hart Fell*

| | |
|---|---|
| **Start/Finish** | A708 1km northeast of Capplegill (NT 151 102) |
| **Distance** | 15km (9½ miles) |
| **Ascent** | 900m (3000ft) |
| **Approx time** | 5½hrs |
| **Terrain** | Grassy hill slopes and ridges (optional stony ravine at start) |
| **Max altitude** | Hart Fell, 808m |
| **Maps** | Landranger 78 (Nithsdale); Explorer 330 (Moffat) |
| **Parking** | Verge parking close to Capplegill farm; but it's more considerate to farm users to use a lay-by under trees 1km east |
| **Variant** | Swatte Fell summit adds 500m (¼ mile) – 10mins |

This route is Southern Uplands all right – but with added surprises. There are the 500m drops on the right all the way around. There is the ridge of Saddle Yoke, an edge that's as sharp as it gets in grass. And there's the Hang Gill scramble at the start. Hang Gill is a ravine with stones and small waterfalls, wild flowers and the bones of unwary goats – because even the wild mountain goats weren't expecting precipices here in Moffatdale. The walls rise on either side, the stream turns a corner, and you're in a trap with a waterfall at the top and no obvious escape.

But there's no need to starve to death slowly while gnawing those ancient goat bones. Simply eat your usual sandwiches below the waterfall, then look on the ravine wall behind you for a short grassy path out onto the open hillside. And after that it's grassy all the way to Hart Fell and grassy all the way home.

Walk along the A702 towards **Capplegill**. Cross the large bridge over the **Blackhope Burn**, but stop at a gate on the right just before the smaller one over the Hang Burn (50 metres east of Capplegill farm). The ravine of Hang Gill is obvious, immediately above the farm. Go up alongside the Hang Burn. Its wide bouldery bed shows the fury of winter storms. In normal conditions, the burn is a mere trickle in the middle.

A gate leads onto open hill at the foot of **Hang Gill**. If there's been a rainstorm and the ravine is full of raging water, it can easily be avoided by grassy slopes on either side – the left (west) side is easier. Otherwise just go up the ravine on grass, stones and boulders. The most interesting line, close to the stream, offers a little easy scrambling on water-worn rocks. The ravine turns right and ends at a small waterfall.

*In Hang Gill – but these rocky steps can be bypassed*

119

Turn sharply back right to a short sheep path that slants up out of the gorge. Head north up the grassy ridge above to a small cairn, and continue in the same direction until an electric fence crosses the ridgeline. On the right, above the drop to Blackhope valley, the fence has a gate.

A broad grass slope leads up. The best way is to stay on its right-hand edge, next to the steep drops of Black Craig – this gives slightly easier going and the finest

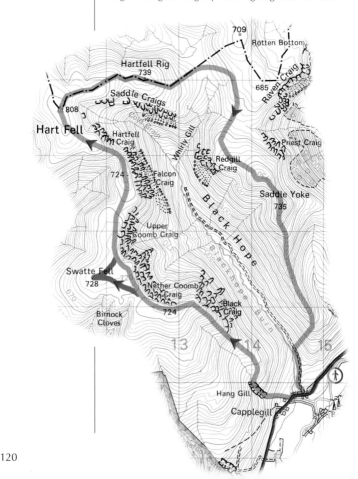

views. Continue up northwest, following the tops of the crags on the right, with a very small path. A fence arrives from the left as the 724m summit **Nether Coomb Craig** is reached.

A short dip leads to the plateau of **Swatte Fell**. Donald-baggers will have to divert left for the actual summit. More relaxed hillgoers will just follow the crag top northwards.

### Diversion to Swatte Fell

For the nondescript summit of Swatte Fell, from the dip slant up left, near the fence on the left, to where it joins a broken wall. The summit is 50 metres to the left, marked by a short transverse wall. Return along the broken wall, which bends left to rejoin the cliff edge above Upper Coomb Craig.

A grass path runs between the fence with its broken wall and the crag top. The third Donald top, **Falcon Craig**, is just to the left of the fence. A steeper slope starts the climb to Hart Fell. Follow the fence to **Hart Fell** trig point with its shelter-cairn surround.

Turn right to head down beside the regional boundary fence. It runs along **Hartfell Rig** and off its end above a broad and rather peaty col. As the fence bends slightly left, keep ahead, down east to cross the tops of streams feeding **Whirly Gill**. Here bend right (southeast) on pathless rough grassland, contouring towards the col to the north of Saddle Yoke. In mist, take care not to carry on contouring past the incised stream that drops northwest from this col to join Whirly Gill. Instead, cross this stream near its top and at once head left, directly uphill, to the shoulder above **Redgill Craig**. There find a small path on up to (Under) **Saddle Yoke**.

The name of **Saddle Yoke** applies properly to the pair of summits and the spectacular gap between them. However, the Explorer map gives the name to the second, more southerly top, with this first one given as Under Saddle Yoke. Needless to say, Under

*On Saddle Yoke*

Saddle Yoke is 10m higher. (Lakeland lovers may like to compare the heights of Hartsop Dodd and High Hartsop Dodd.)

At Under Saddle Yoke the ridge becomes surprisingly sharp. The path shows the way down the steep dip into the saddle. The ridge remains sharp over Saddle Yoke, although there's a fence below on the left to catch you if you should roll off in that direction.

From this point there is the opportunity to contemplate the route of the one-time **Moffat hill race**. The race went straight down this very steep slope to the Blackhope Burn 400m below, splashed through it, and then straight up the even steeper slope opposite to reach Nether Coomb Crag at the start of our walk. This requires rubber-studded hill-running shoes, plus, of course, extremely strong legs.

The path down off Saddle Yoke continues past a small cairn and down southwards. The ridge is now wide, but the drops on the right are still impressive.

Crag and shelf formations near the top of the slope could be meltwater channels (see Walk 12), but it's hard to imagine the Moffat and Blackhope glaciers being this deep, and they look more like **landslips** – erosion by ice or water of softer shale strata below that lets the whole hill slope slide down by 10 or 20 metres.

In a dip, an electric fence crosses the ridge; it has a convenient stile at its highest point. The ridge rises to a hump, then descends south towards Capplegill, now visible below.

A fence crosses the ridge foot. Don't cross, but turn right alongside it, heading down to a track where there is a gate. The track then runs above the Blackhope Burn to the A702 at Blackshope cottage. Turn left along the road to return to the start.

# WALK 21
## *White Coomb*

| | |
|---|---|
| **Start/Finish** | Grey Mare's Tail car park (NT 186 145) |
| **Distance** | 12km (7½ miles) |
| **Ascent** | 750m (2500ft) |
| **Approx time** | 4½hrs |
| **Terrain** | Paths, some peaty, and grassy hills |
| **Max altitude** | White Coomb, 821m |
| **Maps** | Landranger 79 (Hawick); Explorer 330 (Moffat) |
| **Parking** | NTS pay and display |
| **Variant** | Via Dobb's Linn – 13km (8 miles) with 850m (2800ft) of ascent (about 5hrs) |

The main route starts near the much visited Grey Mare's Tail waterfalls. The falls have been celebrated since the Iron Age, when they boasted an ancient 'visitor information centre' in the form of the obscure mounds next to Tail Burn called the Giant's Grave. Well, the official word is 'pagan ceremonies perhaps' – but the National Trust for Scotland (NTS) has mounted its interpretation boards at the exact same spot as the Giant's Grave. And Walter Scott gave an early tourist write-up to Loch Skeen, which the walk passes further on, where

> Eagles scream from isle to shore;
> Down all the rocks the torrents roar;
> O'er the black waves incessant driven,
> Dark mists infect the summer heaven.

Add to the waterfall and lake some grassy ridges smooth enough for golf, and the Southern Uplands' third highest summit – what more could we ask for in a shortish hill day?

An alternative initial section of the route provides an additional attraction. It saves the popular waterfall for the end of the day and takes walkers via the smaller and much more secret ravine Dobb's Linn, where the feet of fleeing Covenanters disturbed scratchy rock markings of 450 million years ago.

An alternative initial section of the walk, via Dobb's Linn, is described below.

◄ Just above the footbridge on the right-hand (east) side of **Tail Burn** is a stone enclosure with interpretation boards – it gives a fully risk-free, but rather distant and obstructed, view of the **Grey Mare's Tail waterfalls**. From here the stone-pitched path heads briefly uphill, before slanting up and across the very steep slopes of **Bran Law** above the gorge and waterfall.

The well-made path arrives above the waterfall top and follows the stream up the valley above, among moraine hummocks. It runs to the right of the stream to arrive suddenly at the outflow of **Loch Skeen**.

You know it's there – but if you have companions who don't, make sure they're walking at the front for the surprise view of Loch Skeen. At 505m altitude, it's 10m higher up than Loch Enoch (Walk 5) and is Southern Scotland's highest loch. At 10m deep it's not a true corrie lochan, as it hasn't been over-deepened by ice, but is held in by the striking moraine field across its foot. The eagles of Walter Scott's verse used to nest on the tiny island, until shot by gamekeepers.

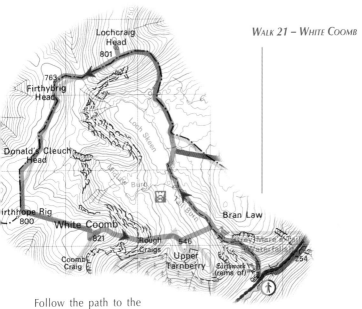

Follow the path to the right around the loch foot, then strike up to the right to join a fence not far above. ▶ This has a peaty path on its left; fence and path cross the crest of the hagland northwards. The

The alternative route by Dobb's Linn joins the main route here.

Grey Mare's Tail

125

*Mid Craig and Lochcraig Head from Loch Skeen*

accompanying fence becomes a fallen wall and runs up the spur of **Lochcraig Head**, turning left to reach the summit. A cairn by the left-hand brink has views down to Loch Skeen. For the true summit, turn away from the brink across the fallen wall and follow a side-fence north for 200 metres. The summit has various puny cairns where different cairn-builders thought the summit was.

The wall leads down southwest across a slightly soggy col (Talla Nick) and up (with a path beside it) to **Firthybrig Head**. The ridge and wall run south then southwest, very smooth and easy, over the imperceptible **Donald's Cleuch Head**. ◀ Keep ahead up the fence and fallen wall, slightly down then up. A fence heads away left, south of east, towards White Coomb. But the summit of **Firthhope Rig** is just slightly further ahead at the fence corner.

*Short-cut – a grass path runs down east here to follow Mid Craig, the fine ridgeline above Loch Skeen, to the loch's outflow.*

Join the fence running along the NTS boundary towards White Coomb. Its lowest point is just down to the right of the true col. It rises to a corner (with the broken wall continuing ahead). Cross a stile on the left, then bear right around the fence corner (in mist, south from the fence corner) to **White Coomb** summit cairn.

Head down east to rejoin the fallen wall. A small path runs beside it down the ridge south of east. There's a steep descent at **Rough Craigs**, where the path is eroding down to bare rock. Below this, the path and fallen wall run out onto a moorland hump. Here they bend left and descend peat ground to Tail Burn. Cross above a minor waterfall to the well-made path beyond. Follow it down above the Grey Mare's Tail waterfalls to the car park.

**Alternative start by Dobb's Linn**
From the car park return to the A708 and head east for 300 metres to cross the bridge over Moffat Water. Head

## DOBB'S LINN

Watch Knowe was a lookout point in Covenanting times – wander left above Dobb's Linn to get views from the brink of Bran Law all up and down Moffatdale. 'Dobb' refers to Halbert Dobson, who hid in the linn below. The moraines and peat around Loch Skeen were good ground for fugitives on foot being pursued on horseback.

*Graptolite fossils (up to 2cm long) from Dobb's Linn*

But Dobb's Linn is important today for its graptolite fossils – scratchy marks that look as if small threaded screws have been pressed into the rock. The name means 'writing', although the only 'letters' are I and V. The writing was read by Charles Lapworth (born 1842), who spent 11 years studying them. Eventually he unravelled not only the complex folding and faulting of the Southern Uplands, but also the time-line of the Ordovician period (which he invented) and the Silurian period. The division between them is still marked by a metaphorical 'golden spike' driven into the shale of Dobb's Linn.

Fossils are best spotted in spring, after winter's fresh erosion and before most of the other geologists arrive. Turn over slaty-looking shale in stream-beds and fresh scree. A 10-minute search should find some. They are in fact little bacterial 'rafts' that dropped into the mud of the ocean that once separated Scotland and England.

The gentle stream gill ahead is a pleasant escape up onto the moor.

If the steep grass is waterlogged and slippery, the little stream slot up to the right, north, from the foot of the waterfall is an easier way up, with shale exposures and graptolites.

up steep grass on the right to find an old path, the former road along the valley. Follow this, above the tarmac road, to cross an eroded stream below a gill. After 1.2km the old path rejoins the road opposite the incised little valley of Dobb's Linn. Cross the road and the valley floor to enter **Dobb's Linn**.

After 400 metres the linn forks. ◄ Turn left on a small goat/geologists' path by the stream to reach the foot of the waterfall, which is a double one, down slabs.

Head up steep grass to the right of the waterfall, zigzagging among small outcrops with rowan trees. ◄ Turn left through bracken, crossing a stream and then the main stream above the waterfall. Head up over shaggy grass to the left of the waterfall stream, crossing it near its top. Continue directly uphill (north) over grassy ground to the small cairn on **Watch Knowe**.

There's a fence just beyond. The col to the north has swampy hags. So once across the fence, turn down left beside it towards the foot of Loch Skeen. Just above the loch the fence bends right, with a peaty path on its left. Continue with the main route from here, following fence and path north.

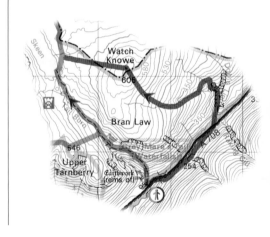

# WALK 22

*White Coomb and Hart Fell*

| | |
|---|---|
| **Start/Finish** | Grey Mare's Tail car park (NT 186 145) |
| **Distance** | 28km (17½ miles) |
| **Ascent** | 1200m (4000ft) |
| **Approx time** | 9½hrs |
| **Terrain** | Paths; some peaty, grassy hills with a few rough sections; 7km road to finish |
| **Max altitude** | White Coomb, 821m |
| **Maps** | Landrangers 78 (Nithsdale) and 79 (Hawick); Explorer 330 (Moffat) |
| **Parking** | NTS pay-and-display |
| **Variant** | Swatte Fell summit adds 500m (¼ mile) – 10mins |

Hart Fell (Walk 20) has the huge hollow of Black Hope, fringed with crag, and a grassy ridgeline all along the top. White Coomb (Walk 21) offers Loch Skeen, the best mountain lake between Loweswater and Loch Lomond. It also gives access to the Grey Mare's Tail, which is one of the best mountain waterfalls anywhere. It's tempting to combine the two of them into this one long hill day.

Go all the way to the top of the tail, and which (rather nastier) part of the horse do you eventually get to? The place called Rotten Bottom is classic Southern Upland terrain. In other words, it's a bit of a bog. A Bronze Age arrow was found up there, and the reason they didn't find the Bronze Age archer was that he probably despairingly fired his last arrow upwards before going 'glug' and sinking into the slime.

A walk in the Southern Uplands and coming home with clean feet isn't part of the bargain. What you will get is comfortable grassy going, crag-ringed hollows, a small lake and a big, big waterfall.

Follow Walk 21 to **White Coomb** summit. For shorter alternatives, use the fine ridge northwest from Loch Skeen outflow or the descent in Walk 21 by Rough Craigs.

Came up by Rough Craigs? Head south for 100 metres to a fence corner. Just around the corner cross a stile on the left and follow the fence down across a shallow col.

map continues on page 132

Return to the fence junction on **Firthhope Rig**. ◄ Turn left on a small path beside the wall and fence, dropping west along a gentle ridge, then more steeply south-west to the wide and well-named col **Rotten Bottom**.

To the left of the main fence is heathy peat, part of the Carrifran Wildwood; to the right of it appears grassy, but some of that grass is a mossy morass. Walkers who cross to the right of the fence will need to skirt 200 metres to the right around the morass. Easier is to stay to the left of the fence, following the old wall and then very old fence remains and traces of path through the heathery peat.

The wall reappears alongside the newer seven-strand fence for the rise to the 685m top above **Raven Craig**. At the top is a three-way fence junction. ◄ Cross a stile, then leave the fences to keep ahead, due west, down a grassy rough slope.

Cross the head of the streams feeding **Whirly Gill** and keep ahead up the slope of **Hartfell Rig**, joining the fence on your right. It leads gently up to the trig point of **Hart Fell**.

Short-cut – turn left along the fence and descend over Saddle Yoke as on Walk 20.

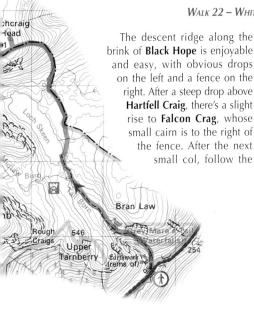

The descent ridge along the brink of **Black Hope** is enjoyable and easy, with obvious drops on the left and a fence on the right. After a steep drop above **Hartfell Craig**, there's a slight rise to **Falcon Crag**, whose small cairn is to the right of the fence. After the next small col, follow the

*Mid Craig, Lochcraig Head and Loch Skeen seen from the east ridge of White Coomb*

*Looking down into Black Hope from Hartfell Rig*

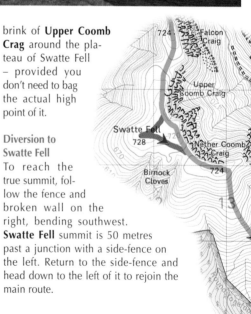

brink of **Upper Coomb Crag** around the plateau of Swatte Fell – provided you don't need to bag the actual high point of it.

**Diversion to Swatte Fell**

To reach the true summit, follow the fence and broken wall on the right, bending southwest. **Swatte Fell** summit is 50 metres past a junction with a side-fence on the left. Return to the side-fence and head down to the left of it to rejoin the main route.

Both ways lead to a grassy col and a small path leading up to the cairn on **Nether Coomb Craig**.

The direct route used in ascent on Walk 20 is scenic, but steep. For a gentler way down, cross the fence alongside the summit – there's a strainer post just down to the left. Head down rough grassy slopes, slightly east of south, on the slight spur-line to the right of Hang Beck (the stream above Hang Gill).

At the 300m contour an electric fence runs across. About 300 metres in from the **Roundstonefoot Burn** and its plantations there's a gate. Here pick up a green tractor-track that slants to the left athwart the slope to arrive above **Capplegill farm**.

Through a gate just above the farm, turn down right on a faint tractor track to meet the farmyard entrance track just above the **A708**.

Turn left along the quiet road for 7km to the Grey Mare's Tail car park.

# WALK 23

*Loch of the Lowes and Ward Law*

| | |
|---|---|
| **Start/Finish** | Loch of the Lowes foot (NT 238 204) |
| **Distance** | 15km (9 miles) |
| **Ascent** | 550m (1900ft) |
| **Approx time** | 4½hrs |
| **Terrain** | Paths and grassy hills |
| **Max altitude** | Ward Law, 594m |
| **Maps** | Landrangers 73 (Peebles) and 79 (Hawick); Explorer 330 (Moffat) |
| **Parking** | At Glen Café on A708 at foot of Loch of the Lowes |
| **Variant** | Turn back at Peniestone Knowe to go by Pikestone Rig and Earl's Hill – 10.5km (6½ miles) with 400m (1300ft) of ascent (about 3½hrs) |

Two hundred years ago, poet James Hogg (the 'Ettrick Shepherd') crossed these hills from his home in Ettrick Glen to meet up with Walter Scott at Tibbie Shiel's – and, perhaps, assignations of a more intimate sort with Tibbie herself. He celebrated his local hill rambles in the poem 'A Boy's Song' and must have enjoyed the green path above Loch of the Lowes just as much as the poetic discourse, not to mention the beer, at the inn below. The walk offers grassy paths and gentle hilltops above a peaceful Borders' glen, as well as two lovely lochs – you don't have to be a poet to go for it here.

Cross the bridge between the two lochs, and at once turn right through a field gate. Cross the field to a tall footbridge and a gate at the northeast corner of **Loch of the Lowes**.

Follow the footpath along the loch edge. Halfway along the eastern shore, a stream, usually dry, has a pronounced debris cone, now grass covered. Here turn uphill, to the right of the dry stream, on what becomes a clear path slanting up south above the loch. The path joins a wider quad-bike track, which contours forward to join a green track above **Riskinhope farm**.

Turn uphill on this old track. It slants up left, but at once turns sharp right and slants up and around the flank of **Peat Hill** above Riskinhope Burn.

At the back of Peat Hill the track crosses a swampy stream. It becomes clear and dry again, running due south to the col on **Pikestone Rig**. Here it meets the SU Way, marked with two waymark posts. ▸

Ignoring SU Way markers on the left and down ahead, turn up to the right, following a quad-bike path up the gentle ridgeline. As the ground levels off, the track fades. Continue across tussocks for the last 400 metres to **Peniestone Knowe**. The summit has a small pool, a fallen wall and a fence junction.

The SU Way running to the left here will be the descent on the shorter return route (see below).

### Short-cut by Pikestone Rig and Earl's Hill

For the shorter route, return down the ridge to the col at **Pikestone Rig**. Keep ahead across the little col onto the SU Way's firm grassy path. This runs along the ridge crest and down over its end. Here it bends down right, zigzagging through a gateway in a wall to reach **Riskinhope**

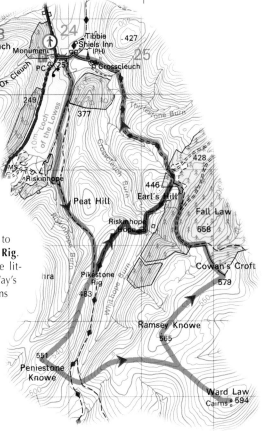

'Hope' is a high hollow between the hills; such places were often used as shieling or summer pasture.

**Hope.** ◀ The ruined house is covered in pink willow herb. Just below, a footbridge crosses **Whithope Burn**.

The wide, clear path slants up the side of **Earl's Hill**. It passes the corner of plantations, then heads through the wide col east of Earl's Hill to a stile into plantations. It passes a signpost, descends gently to cross a stream, and rises briefly to arrive at a forest road.

A few steps left is a gate with cattle grid underneath. Carry on down this track (now back on the main route) to Tibbie Shiels Inn and the walk start.

Turn left following a fence down quite steeply to a wide, wet col. Cross the SU Way and continue to the left of the fence across the wide, damp col and up the spur-line towards Ramsey Knowe. A signpost in the fence marks the lost line of the old path used by James Hogg to get to Tibbie Shiel's.

The slope levels off at Rig Head. In mist it might be advisable to keep following the fence up onto Ramsey

## THE ETTRICK SHEPHERD

James Hogg, sheep farmer, poet and novelist, is commemorated by a statue overlooking the walk start. He was nicknamed the 'Ettrick Shepherd' because he worked as a shepherd (and later a struggling small farmer) in the Ettrick valley. Hogg was born in 1770; his grandfather was the last man in all the Borders to speak with the fairies.

As an unschooled 'peasant poet', Hogg wowed the Edinburgh establishment a generation after Robert Burns. He often used the old path across Pikestone Rig to meet up at Tibbie Shiel's with his friend Walter Scott, to whom he passed on ballads and folk tales.

Hogg's unsettling philosophical novel *Confessions of a Justified Sinner* was admired by Emile Zola among others. Was he any good as a poet? Look up 'A Boy's Song'.

> *Where the pools are bright and deep,*
> *Where the grey trout lies asleep,*
> *Up the river and over the lea,*
> *That's the way for Billy and me.*

Knowe. But the large cairn on Ward Law has been a way-mark since Peniestone Knowe; in clear conditions cross the fence at its corner and contour east to a col at 519m, and here join a tall deer fence. Follow this up to the tall cairn on **Ward Law**.

*Ward Law's northeast cairn before construction of the deer fence*

> The imposing aspect of the **Ward Law cairn** is now diminished by the deer fence (built about 2012) alongside it, but the cairn has been there since Queen Victoria's Jubilee (1887) and will outlast the fence by a few centuries. A second and even finer cairn, now equally fence-hemmed, is 800 metres on down the northeast ridge, and has even better Ettrick views.

There's a ladder stile here, but don't cross it. Return downhill to the left of the fence, and up the rough slope to **Ramsey Knowe**. At its nondescript top, turn right, still alongside the deer fence, although there's now a quad-bike track a little out to the left. Continue northeast along the wide ridgeline to **Cowan's Croft**.

Turn down left following a normal-sized fence. Soon there are plantations on the right. At the slope foot, cross

*Tibbie Shiels Inn, between Loch of the Lowes and St Mary's Loch*

the fence and continue along the edge of the trees. Turn left around the fence corner, joining a wet green track (Captain's Road). After 300 metres this becomes a gravelled forest road, bending down right into the forest.

The apparent path from its top corner follows the line marked on the map, but peters out in pine needles and black peat.

After 600 metres down the road, look out for a small cairn and waymark on the left – they're at a point where a forest ride gives clear views down towards Peat Hill. Fork down left here on a faint path between the trees. After 100 metres the path runs along a slender clearing. Leave this at its bottom corner ahead. ◄ The path slants down under needle-trees to the edge of open ground, and follows this around and left to a signpost on the SU Way.

For the long combination walk over The Wiss, switch here to Walk 24.

Turn down to the right. The path dips to a footbridge, then rises to join a gravelled track. ◄ Turn left, through a gate, to follow the track down the valley side of **Crosscleuch Burn**. The track joins a tarmac driveway, running ahead past **Tibbie Shiels Inn** and over the bridge between the lochs to the A708.

# WALK 24

*The Wiss and St Mary's Loch*

| | |
|---|---|
| **Start/Finish** | Loch of the Lowes foot (NT 238 204) |
| **Distance** | 14.5km (9 miles) |
| **Ascent** | 400m (1200ft) |
| **Approx time** | 5hrs |
| **Terrain** | Paths, grassy hills, and a heathery section descending The Wiss |
| **Max altitude** | The Wiss, 589m |
| **Maps** | Landrangers 73 (Peebles) and 79 (Hawick); Explorer 330 (Moffat) |
| **Parking** | Glen Café on A708 at foot of Loch of the Lowes |
| **Variant** | Start with the initial part of Walk 23, going from Loch of Lowes by Peniestone Knowe and Ward Law, to join Walk 24 after Earl's Hill and continue to The Wiss – 24km (15 miles) with 800m (2600ft) of ascent (7½hrs) |

Yarrow glen has to be the Borders' Lake District, with its two – count them! – lochs. Make the most of them by combining part of Walk 23 with this route for a big day over fairly small hills. The Wiss is quite tough on top, with a heathery couple of kilometres until the grassy sheep-walk of Altrieve Rig is reached. The return is along the lakeside for 5km on the good SU Way path.

▶ Cross the bridge between the lochs, and follow the tarmac lane past **Tibbie Shiels Inn**. Near a phone mast, keep straight uphill on a track marked as the SU Way.

After 2km of gentle but steady climb, a gate is just ahead leading into forest plantations. Immediately in front of this, turn left off the track, up alongside the forest edge. ▶ Where the forest bends away to the right keep ahead up the grassy slope. There's usually a quad-bike track up the first grassy rise to the levelling Long Moor. Here the going is damper and a bit heathery.

Join the forest edge up the next rise, until the fence bends up slightly left. Follow it up to a small gate at the top

For the longer version of the walk, start with Walk 23.

The longer walk arrives here through the gate ahead.

*Ascending The Wiss, with view to White Coomb (Walk 21)*

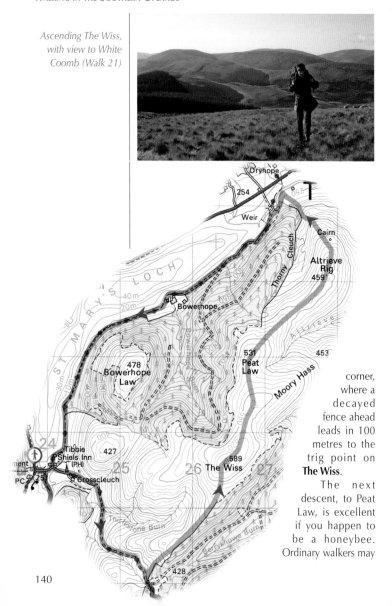

corner, where a decayed fence ahead leads in 100 metres to the trig point on **The Wiss**.

The next descent, to Peat Law, is excellent if you happen to be a honeybee. Ordinary walkers may

140

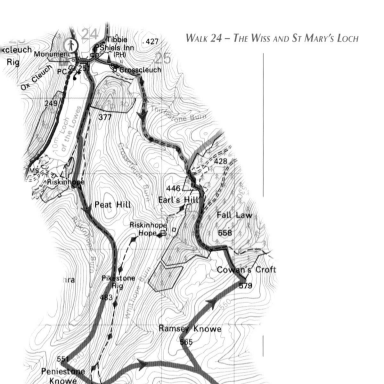

not appreciate the profusion of heather here, so take your time. Follow the decayed fence northeast, past a fence junction. There are path traces to the left of the fence as it leads down to the slight rise of **Peat Law**.

Cross the fence here onto slightly grassier ground. With luck, find quad-bike tracks along the ridgeline of **Altrieve Rig**. Off the ridge end descend slightly left (northwest) to some trees left behind along the edge of clear-felled plantations. Go through the gate here, and

At the end of the Ice Age, St Mary's and the Lowes were a single loch – gravel from stream outflows on either side has separated them.

another through a wall just below, and keep down ahead to the field foot and a gate alongside Yarrow Water.

Turn left, upstream, with the wall on your left. Pass along the foot of the plantations to meet a track near the dam at the foot of **St Mary's Loch**. ◄

The route has now rejoined the SU Way. Turn left along the smooth gravel track, soon running alongside the loch. After 1km bear right on the lower track. In another 500 metres, just before **Bowerhope house**, bear right through a waymarked gate to continue along the grassy loch side to a stile.

The well-made path continues along the loch side, with stiles and the occasional little bridge. After 1km pass the 'Shinglehook' sculpture.

The **Shinglehook** sculpture is a response to the shingle outwash fan from Megget Water on the opposite side; in 10,000 years or so the fan will reach where you now stand and divide the loch into two.

The path continues to a gate at the loch's southeast corner. Follow the shore around to the sailing club. Here pick up a track past Tibbie Shiel's Inn to the lane beyond. Turn right to the bridge between the lochs.

## TIBBIE SHIEL

Tibbie Shiel was a long-time friend and neighbour of the poet James Hogg (see Walk 23). She set up the inn between the two lochs to support her large family after the death of her husband, a mole-catcher. Later in life she was noted as a religious lady, who compelled guests staying on a Sunday to attend kirk worship. However, although not an admirer of Hogg's rhymes ('He wrote a deal o' trash but was a gey sensible man for a' that'), it's rumoured that the young widow Tibbie extended to him favours going beyond the mug of ale and the porridge pot; and at his death, it was she who laid out his body.

Today at the inn folk singing replaces Scots verse. The atmosphere is still relaxed – the inn recently closed for four days because the entire staff was appearing in the local pantomime.

# 4 MANOR HILLS TO THE TWEED

*Above Talla Linnfoots on the approach to Broad Law (Walk 25)*

# INTRODUCTION

The Manor Hills form a great horseshoe facing north to Peebles. The many small summits are linked by high ridgelines. The high-level Thief's Road of the cattle raiders can still be traced, and is followed on Walk 26. Also still in evidence is the route of the later drovers plodding up from Peebles southwards over the tops (Walk 28). The long windy ridges are just as good for present-day walkers, unaccompanied by cows.

The River Tweed is English through Berwick, and forms the national border past Coldstream. But upstream from there to Peebles it's the main drainage of Scotland's Borders region – a wide fertile strath separating the Cheviots from the Southern Uplands proper.

Between Tweeddale and Edinburgh lie the Moorfoots, which some have disparaged for their flat tops, peaty bogs, plantations and windfarms. But nobody can dislike the two volcanic knobbles that erupt out of the Tweed's wide valley. Ruberslaw (Walk 32) is haunted by a hairy-faced holy man of the Covenanting times, and Eildon (Walk 31) is home to the Queen of the Fairies herself.

# WALK 25

*Broad Law*

| | |
|---|---|
| **Start/Finish** | Hearthstanes track end on A701 2km north of Tweedsmuir (NT 109 260) |
| **Distance** | 21km (13 miles) |
| **Ascent** | 800m (2700ft) |
| **Approx time** | 7hrs |
| **Terrain** | Grassy ridges, mostly following fences |
| **Max altitude** | Broad Law, 840m |
| **Maps** | Landranger 72 (Upper Clyde); Explorers 330 (Moffat) and 336 (Biggar) |
| **Parking** | Small pull-in immediately north of the farm track |

Broad Law resembles Broad Cairn on Deeside, and possibly even Broad Peak in the Karakoram, in being rather large (Broad Law is the Southern Uplands' second highest) and also a bit of a sprawly lump. In Broad Law's case the interesting side is the northwestern. Narrow, steep-sided glens run in from the River Tweed, and Mathieside Cairn, perched high above Talla Reservoir, is a well-shaped summit that's the high point of this walk in everything but altitude.

The high-level ('level' is appropriate) stroll along Broad Law's summit ridge is pleasingly easy, and the bandstand-like summit structure may amuse. The going is pathless but still mostly gentle, and fences guide the way, at least as far as the final hill.

▶ Follow the **Hearthstanes** access track across the River Tweed until it bends left towards the farm. Don't cross the bridge to the farm, but take a field gate on the right. Head diagonally up to a gateway in the top right corner onto open hill.

Continue straight uphill, soon crossing a contouring track, and then join the edge of a forest on the right. The

Hearthstanes is marked as 'Hearthstane' on OS maps.

*Broad Law's steep northern slope, seen from Taberon Law*

fence leads to the top of the steep slope, then bends right to cross the minor summit of **Hog Hill**.

Keep following the forest fence along the ridgeline, south then bending southeast over the slight hump of **Manyleith Head**. In the following col the forest fence bears off to the right – keep ahead up the well-defined ridgeline, following posts of an old fence over **Snout Hill** and then up to the top of **Mathieside Cairn**.

On Landranger, this is just the higher south top of Mathieside Cairn.

Here join a proper fence, which after a slight dip leads over Talla Cleuch Head. ◀ It then bends left and drops southeast to a col. Keep following the fence across the col – the tops of eroded gullies on the right look down on Talla Linnfoots. The fence leads east up **Cairn Law** – not a summit, but a fence junction with a handsome cairn on the right.

Behind the bandstand, and marked with snow poles, is a track that leads directly back to Hearthstanes and the walk start.

Take the fence up to the left, following it north on a wide grassy ridge with very pleasant walking to the trig point on **Broad Law**. The 'bandstand' structure, which actually emits radio waves, is over on the left. ◀

*On Cairn Law, looking across Talla valley to Lochcraig Head*

Follow the fence ahead, soon joining a track (marked with snow poles) that leads through a gate in a wall to Broad Law's northeastern radio tower above **Polmood Craig**. Past this join the fence on the left, which leads down across a broad col and up the slopes of Cramalt Craig. After a gate in a crossing fence, the main fence bends right and runs east to the summit cairn on **Cramalt Craig**.

At one time 831m **Cramalt Craig** counted as the walk's second Corbett or Scottish 2500-footer. With the defining col (just crossed on the way from Broad Law) at between 680m and 690m, it lacks the 152m (500ft) of drop for Corbett qualification, although it might just satisfy the 150m (492ft) required of a Marilyn. Currently it features in neither list.

map continues
on page 148

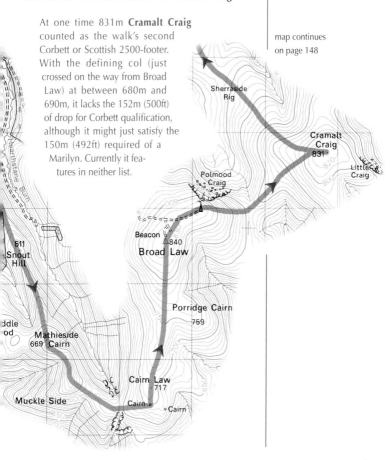

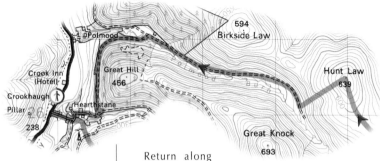

Return along the fence to its bend (above the crossing fence with gate). Keep straight ahead, on the first bit of this section without any guiding fence line, going roughly west then swinging northwest down the grassy, rounded **Sherraside Rig**. The col at its foot is peaty and heathery, with a quad-bike path. This runs up to cross a grouse-shooter's track, and continues up grass to the single fence post at the top of **Hunt Law**.

Descend southwest (aiming for Great Knock opposite) over heathery ground. As the slope steepens drop into a fold in the slope with grassy patches, giving easier going down to the track alongside **Polmood Burn**.

Follow the track downvalley for 2km. Just after the start of plantations on the left-hand side-slope of the valley go through a gate, and in another 100 metres fork left on a rougher track which fords Polmood Burn. The track runs along the foot of plantations, west at first then bending south above the River Tweed. Above Hearthstanes the track bends round left to join the track up **Hearthstane Burn**. Here turn sharp right, following the track down through the farmyard. Bend left on the farm's access track over the Hearthstane Burn, and follow it back across the Tweed to the A701.

# WALK 26

*Manor Head*

| | |
|---|---|
| **Start/Finish** | Manor Water road north of Langhaugh (NT 202 323) |
| **Distance** | 22km (14 miles) |
| **Ascent** | 1100m (3700ft) |
| **Approx time** | 8hrs |
| **Terrain** | Grassy hillsides and ridges, mostly with paths but sometimes rough |
| **Max altitude** | Dollar Law, 817m |
| **Maps** | Landrangers 73 (Peebles) and 72 (Upper Clyde); Explorers 336 (Biggar) and 337 (Peebles) |
| **Parking** | Sheep-nibbled pastures at roadside south of cattle grid under Posso Craig |

At the end of the long Manor glen, the eye is drawn down the folds of converging streams to the white speck of habitation that's the final farm, Manorhead. The circuit of its skyline is a succession of rounded grassy tops, the way marked by fences and by peaty quad-bike paths. The lower, eastern hills are peaty grass and cloudberry; but then the old Thief's Road leads up onto the close-cropped grass of Dollar Law and Pikestone Hill, a walk in the park – but 600m up into the sky.

Head on along the road and turn left over the bridge towards **Langhaugh**. At once fork left off the driveway onto a dirt track. Where this bends left just past the farm, keep ahead on a green track, fording Langhaugh Burn. Head uphill to the left of a plantation, through a gate.

From the plantation's top corner, a faint grassy track heads on up **Langhaugh Hill**. Beyond the slight summit, the track crosses a wide, flat col, and slants up the right flank of **Waddyside Rig**. As the track levels off, bear left to join old decayed fencing, and follow this east over rough ground to the newer fence that crosses **Blackhouse Heights**. ▶

Blackhouse Heights is named Black Cleuch Hill on Explorer maps.

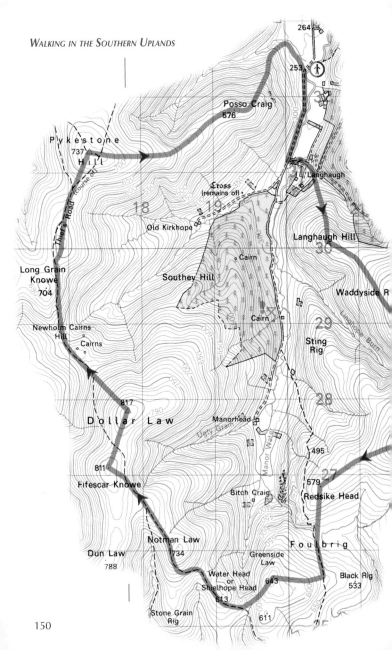

264

253

Posso Craig
576

Pykestone
Hill
737

Thief's Road (course of)

Langhaugh

Cross
(remains of)

Old Kirkhope

Langhaugh Hill

18

19

Cairn

Southey Hill

Waddyside R

Long Grain
Knowe
704

Cairn

29

Landslope Burn

Newholm Cairns
Hill
Cairns

Sting
Rig

817

28

D o l l a r   L a w

Manorhead

Ugly Grain

811

Manor Water

495

Fifescar Knowe

679

27

Bitch Craig

Redsike Head

Notman Law
734

F o u l b r i g

Dun Law
788

Greenside
Law

Black Rig
533

Water Head
or
Shielhope Head
613

Stone Grain
Rig

611

Turn right (south) on a faint path to the left of the fence. The going is grassy across the two tops of **Black Law**, getting rougher as the route descends just south of west along the ridge to **Redsike Head**. At the ridge end turn down left alongside the fence, following it across the main Manor Head col to join a stony track at a gate.

The ridge ahead is peat hagged, so follow the track up left to its highest point, then turn up right on rough grass to rejoin the fence across **Greenside Law**. The summit is off to the right of the fence. Rejoin the fence heading down southwest to a col, with steep drops to Manor valley on the right. Cross the fence to find a green track to the left of it.

This is the **Thief's Road**. The 'thieves' who used the road were reivers of the 16th century, although it probably only became a defined single path 200 years later under the cattle drovers.

*Manor Head from Langhaugh Hill*

151

The path slants up around the left flank of the minor hump **Water Head**, approaches the ridgeline fence in the col beyond, then slants off left again up the flank of **Notman Law**. It passes through the fence at a gate on the shoulder of Fifescar Knowe. As the green track levels off, head up left to the broken wall and old fence along the main ridgeline at **Fifescar Knowe** summit.

Follow fence and wall across short grass north to the trig point on Dollar Law. Bear left and descend beside the fence to a major col, with a hump in it sporting two tall boundary cairns. (A signpost left of the fence here marks the Thief's Road line and a side-path to the left for Stanhope.)

## LORD OF THE MANORS

The grassy, gently undulating Manor Hills are an invitation to fast and prolonged hill-walking. Anyone who completes the circuit from Peebles around the natural horseshoe to Dun Rig, Blackhouse Heights and Dollar Law has passed a lot of grass and seen a lot of peat, and may award themself the title of Lord or Lady of the Manors.

To achieve this circuit, start along Walk 28 from Peebles to Dun Rig, follow the ridges southwest to Blackhouse Heights, then continue on this walk to Pykestone Hill. Continue north over the Scrape to the pass at Dead Wife's Grave. A rough path leads down south of east and joins a forest track down to Hallmanor. Finish along the Tweed past Neidpath Castle (Walk 27).

*Manor valley to Dollar Law, seen from the southwest fort on Cademuir Hill*

You'll have covered 44km and 1400m of ascent (27 miles and 4600ft) – by the reckoning used in this book, about 14 hours, although anyone attempting it will presumably be faster than this book's reckonings.

From the col beyond the tall cairns, a path to the right of the fence becomes a green track slanting up the right-hand (east) flank of Long Grain Knowe to rejoin the ridgeline fence. Head north on short grass over the slight hump of Grey Weather Law to the trig point on Pykestone Hill.

Descend east on a grassy slope, which gets shaggier as it turns more northwards at some tiny peat pools and heads to the ridge end above **Posso Craig**. A few low old cairn remains mark the line northeast to the top of the spur running down above the rocky scree scar of Posso Craig. At the ridge foot, turn right along a track to rejoin the valley road.

# WALK 27
*Cademuir Hill and the Tweed*

| | |
|---|---|
| **Start/Finish** | Kingsmeadows, Peebles (NT 251 401) |
| **Distance** | 12.5km (7½ miles) |
| **Ascent** | 300m (1000ft) |
| **Approx time** | 4hrs |
| **Terrain** | Good paths; one short steep descent |
| **Max altitude** | Cademuir fort, 407m |
| **Maps** | Landranger 73 (Peebles); Explorer 337 (Peebles) |
| **Public transport** | Good bus links to Edinburgh and nearby towns |
| **Parking** | Kingsmeadows car park at south end of Tweed Bridge |

Cademuir is the hill that in its small way has everything. Its hill fort is a good one, with actual masonry remains and chevaux-de-frise, which are spiky stones placed in a hidden ditch just where they might make you fall off your horse and hurt yourself. Its grassy summit has big-hill drops around it and views around the entire range of the Manors – it doesn't just leave you wanting more, but displays the rather bigger hills on which you can do that 'more'.

After the small hill comes the big river. The walk along the Tweed is among wild flowers below great slopes of oak. Finally there is the climb up the 30m of stone steps to the battlements of Neidpath Castle.

The John Buchan Way signs lead right up onto Cademuir. ◀

From the car park entrance, turn right towards Tweed Bridge and head to a road junction with an oak tree in the middle. Behind it, a tarred path runs uphill, with a sign for the John Buchan Way. ◀

At the path's top, turn right for 150 metres along Chambers Terrace to a T-junction. Turn left, uphill, after 30 metres forking left into a tarmac path that starts as a tunnel under trees. At its top, turn right along a tarmac path running just above a lane. After 300 metres, at the lane end, turn up left following a sign for Cademuir Hill and the John Buchan Way. Opposite a lodge dated 1884, another

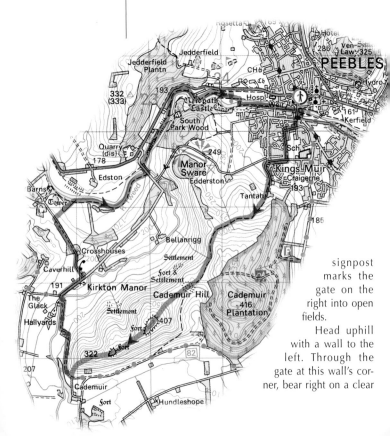

signpost marks the gate on the right into open fields.

Head uphill with a wall to the left. Through the gate at this wall's corner, bear right on a clear

waymarked path, slanting gently uphill. After 1km the path turns more steeply uphill, then contours across a steep slope into the col between the two summits of **Cademuir Hill**. ▶

*John Buchan Way on Cademuir Hill*

The lumpy ground here is an ancient settlement.

Here the route leaves the John Buchan Way, whose markers fork off down left. Instead, keep ahead up the crest to the **fort** at the 407m summit, which has some stonework rings round it. This is Cademuir's 'real' summit, although the actual highest point is in a nasty plantation 2km east.

Steep slopes drop south. Follow their brink down southwest to the final fort, which is impressive with its masonry remains and chevaux-de-frise (spiky stones as obstacles to horsemen). Continue down the ridge on small grass paths. It steepens, to finish at a lane near **Cademuir farm**.

Turn right for 1km to cross Manor Water and turn right. After 400 metres reach **Kirkton Manor** with its church. Just past this, a gravel driveway on the left starts between stone gateposts at a lodge.

Follow the driveway for 1km. Now a stile on the right is waymarked 'Tweed Walk'. A wide green track leads to

*Neidpath Castle and the River Tweed*

the **River Tweed**. Turn right, downstream, on a good path for 1km to a stone-arched road bridge.

Cross this, and just before the piers of a former railway turn right through a gate. The wide, well-made path rises onto the old rail-bed. After 300 metres a gate on the right gives access onto a smaller path through riverside meadows. After 800 metres a fine viaduct crosses the Tweed. The path passes under its arch (or steps lead up onto the bridge for the views along the river). Continue on the same, left, bank, to pass below **Neidpath Castle**.

Fancy some history with your hill? A small side-path leads up to **Neidpath Castle**, which has a fairly small entry charge. This was the stronghold of Sir Symon Fraser, who defeated the English three times in one day at Roslin in 1303, defended Tweeddale for Robert the Bruce, and was hanged, drawn and quartered with a garland of periwinkle around his head in 1312.

Mary Queen of Scots stayed in the place, and Oliver Cromwell's forces knocked it down with cannon in 1650 from across the river. 'Old Q', the fourth Duke of Queensberry, later owned the castle and distressed the Wordsworths by felling trees there in 1795 to fund his London lifestyle, supposedly including a small harem of mistresses.

The main path passes below the castle to Peebles riverside park. Recross the Tweed by a metal footbridge and continue downstream to the Bridge of Tweed. A ramp rises to the roadway above, but the adventurous can regain the car park by passing along a narrow ledge under the bridge arch next to the water.

## WALK 28
*Glen Sax Circuit*

| | |
|---|---|
| **Start/Finish** | Kingsmeadows, Peebles (NT 251 401) |
| **Distance** | 26km (16 miles) |
| **Ascent** | 1000m (3300ft) |
| **Approx time** | 8½hrs |
| **Terrain** | Grassy and heathery ridges, with paths |
| **Max altitude** | Dun Rig, 742m |
| **Maps** | Landranger 73 (Peebles); Explorer 337 (Peebles) |
| **Public transport** | Good bus links to Edinburgh and nearby towns |
| **Parking** | Kingsmeadows car park at south end of Tweed Bridge |
| **Variant** | Finish by the Tweed and Neidpath Castle – 27.5km (17 miles) with 950m (3200ft) of ascent (about 9hrs) |

'Contranatando incrementum' – we increase by swimming against the flow. This is the motto of the town of Peebles, taken from its river salmon. Fighting the English and carrying away their cows is what toughened up the people of Peebles. Walking around the steep sides of Glen Sax, along those cow-thief paths, will strengthen the legs and the character. Manors, as they say, maketh Man – and hill-walking Woman equally.

The town's tough-riding tradition continues in its midsummer Beltane Festival, with horsemen splashing through the river and circling the bounds of the town. But in hot heathery August, the paths are fast, the ground is hardly boggy at all, and the walk to the Tweed could almost be called mild-Manored.

As optional end-of-day relaxation, there's an alternative finish that involves a stroll back along the banks of the Tweed and one last climb up the stone stairway of splendid Neidpath Castle.

Here we have Drovers Way (right) and Gallow Hill (left), recalling that this was a route for cows both stolen and legit.

Cross into Springhill Road, following it southeast. It passes a useful Spar shop and becomes Glen Road. ◄ The street ends with a small parking pull-in on the left, before a green sign pointing ahead for Yarrow. The wide path drops into Gypsy Glen, where it follows the wooded stream downstream for 100 metres before crossing on a footbridge. Now it heads uphill and through a plantation between old dry-stone walls about 30 metres apart.

## THE DROVERS

Every autumn, starting soon after Bonnie Prince Charlie's rebellion and continuing until the building of the railways, 100,000 cows plodded up this path. Gathered from the whole of the Highlands the small black cattle walked south, some to the marts of Crieff and Falkirk but others trekking the length of England to the fields of Norfolk. There they'd be rested and fattened before becoming food for London or salt beef for Wellington's armies.

The cattle covered 12 miles a day, with the tough drovers and their dogs sleeping in the heather wrapped in their woollen plaids. High paths through the hills offered routes that were gentler to the hooves and unobstructed by farmland with its walls, gates and possessive farmers. And no need for motorway service areas – the cows could eat as they went along.

The wide-spaced walls beside the paths, up to 50 metres apart on Kailzie Hill, are an indication of old drove roads. They were to stop the cows from ravaging the moorland grazings too far on either side. The interpretation board at Gypsy Glen conveys the scene, except that the hill path, from wall to wall, would have been churned to black peat and cow pats.

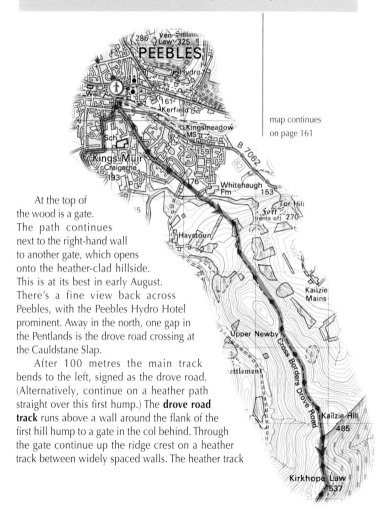

map continues on page 161

At the top of the wood is a gate. The path continues next to the right-hand wall to another gate, which opens onto the heather-clad hillside. This is at its best in early August. There's a fine view back across Peebles, with the Peebles Hydro Hotel prominent. Away in the north, one gap in the Pentlands is the drove road crossing at the Cauldstane Slap.

After 100 metres the main track bends to the left, signed as the drove road. (Alternatively, continue on a heather path straight over this first hump.) The **drove road track** runs above a wall around the flank of the first hill hump to a gate in the col behind. Through the gate continue up the ridge crest on a heather track between widely spaced walls. The heather track

Kailzie's cairn is in the heather to the right of the path.

map continues on page 162

leads onto **Kailzie Hill**, and briefly alongside forestry plantations on its left. ◄

The wide path, with fence to its left, runs up to the cairn on **Kirkhope Law**. It continues, with fence on its left, to **Birkscairn Hill** with its large cairn.

At the foot of the next descent ignore a green footpath signpost, which marks the departure of the drove road towards Yarrow, but stay ahead on the main ridge path to the right of the fence. The cairn on **Stake Law** is a fine lunch-stop viewpoint 20 metres left of the path.

In a few more steps the fence turns away to the right. The path follows some rotten old fence posts across the next shallow col, where it threads through a peat hag. The fence rejoins the path for the rise to the trig on **Dun Rig**.

The path descends over short heather with the fence on its left. In the next shallow col the ground becomes 'southern Manors' – much wetter, with peat, cotton grass and cloudberry. A little above the col, the path bends to the right away from the fence, slanting westwards. It disappears just before it comes to a fence, which you follow down north towards Middle Hill (**Glenrath Heights**). On the way down to the col the path re-forms, and the ground becomes easier 'northern Manors' with heather again.

With the guiding fence on your left, cross **Middle Hill**. Keep following the fence northwards, with a gate in a cross fence, to the very minor rise of **Broom Hill**.

Here turn left, northwest, still with a fence on your left, for the marked dip and rise to **Stob Law**. The tiny cairn is 50 metres to the right of the fence and not at the highest point.

In the following col, a quad-bike track diverts away from the fence around the northeast flank of Glenrath Hill. The wheelmark track rejoins the fence to continue north over **Canada Hill** and then descend northwest. The track is 20 metres to the right of the fence for this steepish descent.

The fence becomes a wall on the way down. Rejoin it at the top corner of a plantation, where a small gate passes through it. Go down a faint grass track to the left of the plantation, through a gate.

At the slope foot the plantation turns into a birchwood. A gate on the right gives access into it. Ignore the faint track ahead, but turn left

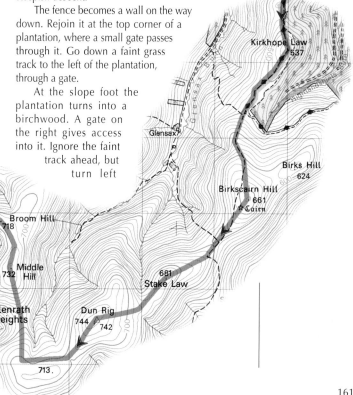

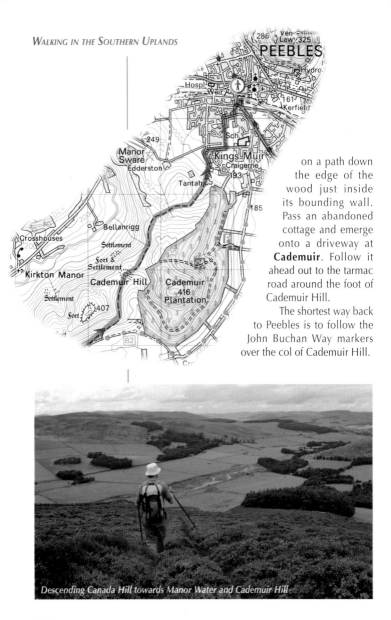

on a path down the edge of the wood just inside its bounding wall. Pass an abandoned cottage and emerge onto a driveway at **Cademuir**. Follow it ahead out to the tarmac road around the foot of Cademuir Hill.

The shortest way back to Peebles is to follow the John Buchan Way markers over the col of Cademuir Hill.

*Descending Canada Hill towards Manor Water and Cademuir Hill*

*On Cademuir Hill, looking back to Stob Law*

▶ Cross the small road and turn right on a path beside it, heading along the foot of Cademuir's steep slope.

After 1km, at a 'bumpy road' sign, the green path slants left up the slope. It has a wall below it as it reaches the col in the middle of **Cademuir Hill**. Follow the way-marked path along the col. As the ground rises ahead, the path contours left across a steep slope, then slants gradually downhill, northeast, to a gate with signpost.

Here turn down left, alongside a high wall, until a gate leads into the lane on the right. Follow this down for 300 metres, then turn right on a tarmac path under trees running just above another lane. After another 300 metres, turn left across the lane and down another tarmac path.

The path joins a downhill street. Take the first turning on the right, Chambers Terrace, and after 150 metres turn down left on a walled tarmac path. It leads down to the road junction at the end of the Tweed Bridge, with the Kingsmeadows car park just to the right.

For a longer but prettier return, switch here to follow Walk 27 back to Kingsmeadows.

# WALK 29
*Lee Pen and Windlestraw Law*

| | |
|---|---|
| **Start/Finish** | Innerleithen (NT 333 368) |
| **Distance** | 27km (17 miles) |
| **Ascent** | 1050m (3500ft) |
| **Approx time** | 9hrs |
| **Terrain** | Grassy hillsides and ridges, mostly with faint paths; forest track and riverside path to finish |
| **Max altitude** | Windlestraw Law, 659m |
| **Maps** | Landranger 73 (Peebles); Explorer 337 (Peebles) |
| **Public transport** | Bus X62 (Edinburgh–Galashiels) |
| **Parking** | Car park, Leithen Road, on the west bank of Leithen Water |
| **Variants** | After descending from Lee Pen shortcut back by Leithen Water – 13km (8 miles) with 600m (1900ft) of ascent (about 4¼hrs); skip the top of Windlestraw Law (save 3km (1½ miles) and minimal ascent) |

The Moorfoots are widely recognised as southern Scotland's least enticing hills. The wide, near-level plateau soaks up rainfall and grows tussock grass, bent heather and sphagnum moss. To this mix humans have added blackened fence posts and broken bits of wire – as well as, on a larger scale, spruce groves and a windfarm.

But in the south, above Innerleithen, streams have carved a better-drained terrain. Windlestraw Law, the range's high point, is generously grassy, with just a patch of peat (on the southwest summit) left in for atmosphere. Across Leithen Water, Lee Pen is small but steep, peat-free and has a healing spring seeping from its side above Innerleithen.

Head upstream (**Leithen Water** is on your right) to the second turning on the left, The Strand, signed for St Ronan's Wells. Wiggle up into Wells Brae to reach the small museum.

The pavilion museum at the former spa of **St Ronan's Wells** describes Innerleithen's boom-town time in the 19th century, when it was a source of bottled fizzy water. The name was attached by Walter Scott, who needed to call the water source something so that he could use it as the title of the novel he was writing. Of 12 available Saint Ronans, the one featured is Ronan of Iona, who drove the Devil out of the Leithen valley. The museum is free, but with limited opening hours – there's also a herb garden.

To the left of the former spa take an uphill path into woods. Fork left up the main path. Soon it contours to the left above a broken wall to meet the tarmac access track of the nearby radio mast. Follow this track up to a bench at the ridge crest.

Ignore a gate ahead, but take the wide path up the crest, with a wall on your left. After a plantation on the left and a couple of field gates, the path zigzags up the steep stony end of **Lee Pen** to the ladder stile at its summit.

The path continues ahead (northwest), with a wall on its left, over the slight rise of **Lee Burn Head** then up Black Knowe. ▶ Cross a ladder stile to the wall corner at **Black Knowe** summit.

'Black' indicates heathery, as against grass-covered Whitehope Law on the other side of Leithen Water.

*Ascending Lee Pen*

*Looking up Leithen Water from Colquhar farm*

Descend northeast, with luck finding a quad-bike track down the spur into the Leithen valley. At the spur foot, bear right, down beside a walled enclosure, to the elderly footbridge at **Colquhar farmhouse**. A lump of masonry, remains of a pele tower, rises among the farm steadings to the left of the stream. Make your own judgement on the footbridge – the river is small and can usually be crossed with dry feet.

### Short-cut by Leithen Water

Lee Pen is the best hill hereabouts, and the walk can be turned into a less demanding half day by returning to Innerleithen from Colquhar. The green track of the original road runs up to the left of the tarmac for nearly 1.5km. Rejoin the road for another 1.5km, and just before the golf clubhouse turn up left on a forest track. Through a gate this bends right to a signpost. Fork down right on a wide stony path signed to Innerleithen.

Caddon Head

Windlestraw
Law
659

Glentress
251

Dod Hill
·427

Bareback Knowe
505

657

Tower
(rems of)
Colquhar

202

Glede Knowe
591

Caberstongrains

543 37
Scawd Law

255

Settlement

The Common

178.1

Settlement

Priesthope
Hill
549

Priesthope
(ruin)
Cairn

Cairn Hill
·499

Weir

Cairn

469
Kirnie Law
Tower

Old
Caberston

Settlement

Pirn Craig
258

Fort

The Kirna

Walkerburn

·rklands

158

Sch

Nether Pirn
146

Weir

133

dismantled railway

135

INNERLEITHEN

West Bold

Haugh-head

144

Cemy

Alternatively, fork up left for a path to Pirn Craig fort just above – view over Innerleithen and some sculptures.

The path runs above the golf course then through plantations. With Leithen Water just below, fork down right to a stone bridge over the river. ◄ Turn left for 200 metres to the car park.

To continue the full-length walk over Windlestraw, turn right on the green track above the road for 50 metres, then left through a field gate. With wall and then fence on your left, head up into the hollow of the **Hope Burn**. After a gate at the fence corner, cross the stream on the left onto an old path on its north side. This heads upstream, then slants up left above a well-built stone sheep enclosure. The path zigzags up to the col behind (east of) **Dod Hill**.

Turn up right on a grassy quad-bike trail to the right of a fence. The fence leads up over the slight levelling of **Bareback Knowe** and on towards the southwest top of Windlestraw Law.

### Short-cut omitting Windlestraw Law

The northeast top of Windlestraw Law, with the trig point, is the Moorfoot high point (659m). To gain the final 2m of height involves an extra 3km on the walk. Those who take in the trig get to avoid the peaty plateau and gain a pleasant rounded ridgeline between the two tops.

On the other hand, it's suggested that on a multi-top hill, it's enough to get your head above the topmost point. Supposing you're 2m tall, the southwest top of Windlestraw (657m) is all you need.

Those who subscribe to this cop-out can simply head on up the fence. As the plateau levels, the trail fades away into a small desert of starved grass and bare peat. Advance to a fence junction and turn left across the actual high point of Windlestraw southwest top to the fine cairn just beyond.

To continue on the main route, which takes in Windlestraw's true top and trig point, from Bareback Knowe head on up the steeper slope until the vegetation gets a bit less harshly heathery then strike out to the left. The rough going gives way to grassland with occasional

small stonefields, staying just below the peat-hags of the gentler slopes above. In the col between Windlestraw's two tops join the ridgeline fence, with a small path.

Follow the fence and path left to the trig point on **Windlestraw**. Return, and follow the path and fence up to the large cairn on Windlestraw's southwest top.

Descend south over rough grass, easing to the right to join a fence descending towards Scawd Law. After the col, a faint wheelmark track runs to the right of the fence line over **Scawd Law**. ▸ The track continues southwards along a well-defined ridge.

At a wall gate, there is the option to strike down to the right through steep heather for a short-cut – not recommended. Instead take the faint path ahead along a heathery tree gap to **Cairn Hill**. ▸

A rough path runs down south in a narrow tree gap. ▸ At the 300m contour meet the end of a timber track. (Meanwhile the tree gap continues down southwards – another nasty short-cut line.) Turn right, contouring then going gently downhill to a hairpin bend and a crossing of **Walker Burn** at the head of its narrow valley.

*On Bareback Knowe, looking back across Leithen valley*

The faint track is marked as a vehicle track on recent Explorer mapping, but is much too faint to qualify as one.

What is it with this Explorer 337? There's no radio mast on Cairn Hill.

Again, the Explorer map considers this a vehicle track.

Just across the stream, turn left on a smaller track signposted for Walkerburn. In 800 metres, this emerges into an open field above the stream. At the next field gate, take a smaller gate on the left for a well-built path (a Tweed Trail) running alongside the stream into Walkerburn. At a farm, bear right through a waymarked gate above a long shed to arrive in the main street in **Walkerburn** (A72).

Cross into Caberston Road opposite. Where it bends left, turn right through a kissing gate to the bank of the **River Tweed**. Head upstream on a gravelly track, which becomes a wide enclosed path – or walk on the grassy riverbank itself.

After 1.5km pass under a former railway bridge, then turn up onto the tarmac cycle path arriving across that bridge. Follow it into **Innerleithen**, but where the cycle path bends right keep ahead on a path along the edge of the houses. At its end, turn right along Princes Street. At the main A72, turn left over Leithen Water, and right in Leithen Road, which leads to the car park at the walk start.

# WALK 30

*Three Brethren and Minch Moor*

| | |
|---|---|
| **Start/Finish** | A708 Yarrowford (NT 407 299) |
| **Distance** | 21km (13½ miles) |
| **Ascent** | 750m (2500ft) |
| **Approx time** | 6½hrs |
| **Terrain** | Wide, smooth paths |
| **Max altitude** | Minch Moor, 567m |
| **Maps** | Landranger 73 (Peebles); Explorer 337 (Peebles) and 338 (Galashiels) |
| **Parking** | A708 lay-by at Yarrowford |
| **Variant** | After Brown Knowe turn immediately down Minchmoor Road – 15km (9½ miles) with 550m (1800ft) of ascent (about 5hrs) |

The Minch Moor is one of the oldest roads in the Borders, recently seeing new traffic as one of the better upland stretches of the Southern Upland Way. The good paths and fairly low altitude make this one of the most comfortable hill walks, and the triangle from Yarrowford offers various short-cuts off the ridge if tiredness or storms set in. Otherwise, just enjoy the way the path switches from one side of the ridge to the other, unfolding new Border valleys all the way along. The forested western end is a bit less delightful, but Minch Moor summit offers a clipped-heather sculpture, a fairy well and new views to the west.

Head east for 100 metres and cross the road into a track, with a sign indicating that Broadmeadows Youth Hostel isn't a hostel any more. The track bends right past a duck pond; then head up left between houses and fork right. The track contours to the right (east) from fields into trees. As it rises towards the cottage that used to be **Broadmeadows** Youth Hostel, fork off right on a waymarked path.

The path contours below the house, then turns up left alongside a stream hollow, with the ruins of an old mill. The path passes up between house and stream to a field gate. Through this, turn right across a footbridge and head along a muddy path with duckboards just above a wall.

At the wall corner ignore a waymark pointing left, and turn right briefly to a stony track. Follow this up to the left, onto the hill and across a wide, flat col north of **Foulshiels Hill**. The Three Brethren cairns are seen

*Three Brethren, the 500-year-old cairns overlooking the Tweed valley*

ahead on the left, but stay on the track as it dips to cross a stream, then rises to a gate with stile.

Keep ahead on a faint path for 200 metres, then turn up left on a small stony track. It runs directly uphill to the three cairns, gate and white trig point at **Three Brethren**.

SU Way markers now guide until the turning point on Minch Moor.

Turn left on the wide, smooth SU Way path. ◄ It runs to the right of a wall, just inside a felled area that is regrowing into a wild spruce wood. Exit by a gate and stile, and shortly ignore a ladder stile on your left. ◄

Over this stile is the first of several possible short-cuts back to Broadmeadows.

The smooth green path continues to the right of the wall, along the top of north-facing slopes of **Broomy Law**, with long views. The path crosses to the southern flank of the ridge and runs above a strip of mixed pine and broad-leaf trees to a stile in a col. ◄

Down left here is another short-cut back to Yarrowford.

This is **Four Lords Lands**. The Three Brethren mark the lairdships of Yair, Philiphaugh and Selkirk, and the four here are Yair and Philiphaugh again, with Traquair and Harden of Yarrow.

Keep following the SU Way up the stiffish climb ahead to the cairn on **Brown Knowe**. Over a stile, continue down ahead to a path junction with sign-post. Back left is the Minchmoor Road, a green path that will be your eventual descent route to Yarrowford. ◄ Continue ahead, as the wide path enters plantations. It runs through a wide tree gap to cross a

Take this now for the shorter variant route back to Yarrowford.

smooth forest road. Now the trees close in, and the path is muddy with a firm stony base.

The path emerges from the trees at a signpost and bench. Up left is Minch Moor summit, but for now continue ahead. The wide path descends gently around the hill's northern flank.

> An interpretation board marks the **Cheese Well**, a spring where offerings of cheese and butter were traditionally left for the fairy folk. These are replaced today by small cash donations. The SU Way rangers have asked walkers not to leave food offerings – presumably it only encourages the fairies.

In another 200 metres, a cleared area below the path has oval shapes designed to be viewed through a sculptural eye-hole. Just ahead, the path divides, with the left fork being the continuing SU Way. ▸

Opposite the sculpture a rough path turns uphill, and this is your route to the summit of Minch Moor. Be alert for descending mountain bikers as the narrow path runs up through heather, with scattered trees to its right, to reach a wider path on the level plateau above. Turn right to the nearby summit cairn on **Minch Moor**.

It's possible here to continue down the SU Way to Traquair, provided that the person with the car keys returns to Yarrowford.

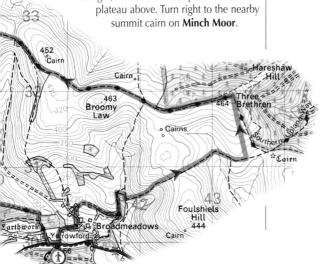

*Heading down Minchmoor Road into Yarrow glen*

Return along the wide path, forking right at the junction you passed previously, and descend to the stile and signpost on the main SU Way path. Retrace your steps through the plantations to the signpost at the top of the **Minchmoor Road**.

Fork right on the gently descending path. After 2km a wall is on your left, and the path goes through two gates along a col.

## WALLACE'S TRENCH AND NEWARK TOWER

In the Middle Ages, Ettrick and Yarrow were tree covered and wild. William Wallace used the area as a refuge and base for attacking the English, and was declared Guardian of Scotland at Selkirk in 1298. On Brown Knowe a faint earthwork, Wallace's Trench, is where he assembled his war-band.

As walkers descend the Minchmoor Road, Newark Tower is glimpsed in the distance where Ettrick and Yarrow Waters converge. Under the Stewart kings Ettrick and Yarrow were a royal hunting forest, and the tower was built as the king's hunting lodge. But in the reiving times it was the stronghold of the Scotts of Buccleuch. They were very effective local warlords, to the extent that their descendant Duke of Buccleuch is now one of the UK's largest landowners. It is possible to walk to Newark Tower from the duke's later and more comfortable residence at Bowhill during Bowhill's summer opening times.

The wide green path now runs along the north flank of Hangingshaw Rig before reaching the top of mixed woodland. Turn left along the wood top, through several waymarked gates. After 800 metres, turn down right through another waymarked gate to the top of a track. This descends quite steeply through the wood. At a track junction keep ahead down a stepped footpath to a street end. This runs ahead through **Yarrowford**, and past its pillarbox-red village hall, to arrive at A708 opposite the parking pull-off.

# WALK 31
*Eildon Hills and the Tweed*

| | |
|---|---|
| **Start/Finish** | Market cross, Melrose (NT 547 340) |
| **Distance** | 22.5km (14 miles) |
| **Ascent** | 750m (2500ft) |
| **Approx time** | 7hrs |
| **Terrain** | Steep stony paths on Eildon; good paths and tracks elsewhere |
| **Max altitude** | Eildon Mid Hill, 422m |
| **Maps** | Landranger 73 (Peebles) and (briefly) 74 Kelso; Explorer 338 (Galashiels) |
| **Public transport** | Frequent buses from Edinburgh and Berwick; buses from Newton St Boswells allow a linear walk |
| **Parking** | Gibson Park, west of Melrose centre |
| **Variant** | Omit two sections: Eildon Hill North; and Dryburgh Abbey to Mertoun Bridge loop – 15.5km (9½ miles) with 650m (2200ft) of ascent (about 5hrs) |

Eildon is a sticky-up hill of a mere 450m, but what it sticks out of is the broad Tweed valley, so there are huge views in all directions. 'Eildon' should perhaps be 'the Eildons', for this was Roman Trimontium ('the triple-hill'). History? Scotland's largest hill settlement and a Roman signal station. Mystery? King Arthur's buried inside, as he is within all such sudden mini-mountains. But keeping him company in there is the Queen of Elfland.

On the northern slopes, back in the 13th century, Thomas the Rhymer had his wicked way with her under the rowan tree. Geology? Volcanic, as any geologist would expect – pink lava with gas-bubble holes.

Looking down from Eildon onto the bends of Tweed – this is very fine. But looking back up at Eildon from the Tweed is also good. Dryburgh Abbey is a contemplative spot, hemmed in with trees and silence. Its groomed lawns belie the time when it was a busy commercial and cultural centre, and the day in 1544 when the Earl of Hertford came murdering and burning on behalf of Henry VIII. The shorter version of the walk turns back here. The full route wanders Tweedside down to Mertoun Bridge, then follows Tweedside back up again to St Boswells. Water crowfoot trails in the brown river, and every half mile has its heron.

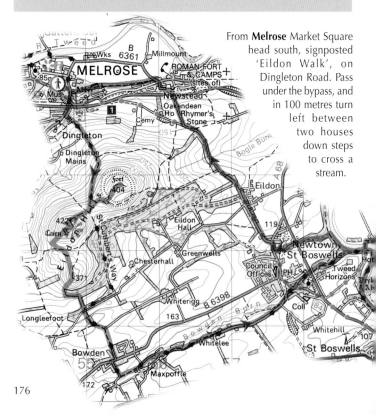

From **Melrose** Market Square head south, signposted 'Eildon Walk', on Dingleton Road. Pass under the bypass, and in 100 metres turn left between two houses down steps to cross a stream.

The path rises in wooden steps, then up field edges, to the foot of open heather slopes on Eildon Hill North. Here it bends right to slant gradually up around the hill to the wide col between North and Mid hills. This could well be the path that the Queen of Elfland leads Thomas up in the ballad…

*Eildon Mid Hill from St Cuthbert's Way path above Melrose*

> And see not ye that bonny road,
> That winds about the fernie brae?
> That is the road to fair Elfland,
> Where thou and I this night maun gae.
> *Ballad of True Thomas*

Turn left up a winding path to the cairn on **Eildon Hill North**. ▶ From the top, there is a view down onto the fort enclosure on the plateau on the south slope and of much surrounding countryside. Descending, there is the option to take a smaller, more direct path back to the col.

Omitting Eildon Hill North saves about ½hr.

177

Go straight across the col and up **Eildon Mid Hill** opposite. The right-hand path is less eroded, spiralling up the north slope to the summit trig point.

*A more direct descent south is steep, loose, and eroding.*

A path leads down southwest, past the remains of an ancient cairn and down the steep heathery spur. ◄ At the foot of the steep heather a waymark post marks a path running across left. Follow any path southeast and up to the small cairn on **Eildon Wester Hill**.

Direct descent south is very steep, so take a small path down slightly south of west, aiming for the right-hand corner of a wood below. Beside this wood corner cross a stile and turn left along a field edge, then bend left on a path just below the wood.

*From here to the Tweed footbridge, further on, is waymarked as St Cuthbert's Way.*

Once through a gate into trees ahead, turn down right on a path with wooden steps. At the wood foot, go down across a track to a footbridge. ◄ Follow a path with more steps up a woodland strip ahead. At the wood top, take a grass path between widely spaced hedges down to the edge of **Bowden**. Keep ahead through a play park to the main street at the stone building around the old village pump.

Turn right for 50 metres, then left in a road signed for Bowden Kirk. After 250 metres the road bends right; here take a hedged path on the left. Keep ahead on this main path, which after 800 metres drops to a footbridge over **Bowden Burn**, then runs up to the right of it to join the corner of a lane. Follow this ahead for 1.5km to meet a main road at the edge of **Newton St Boswells**.

Cross into the lane opposite, rising to a junction at a stone cottage. Turn left (signed to the river, and way-marked by both St Cuthbert and the Border Abbeys). The lane bends right and drops under a high bridge carrying the A68. Just before this bridge, fork right in a wide path.

After a footbridge, keep ahead at a misleading sign-post on a path through blackthorn thickets, then rise onto a high bank above the **River Tweed**. Descend more steps to the green suspension bridge across the big river.

Once across, a romantic Temple of the Muses is up on your left. But turn right, joining a lane and keeping ahead to the entrance to **Dryburgh Abbey**.

### Short-cut omitting the Tweed

Returning to the start from this point saves 1½hrs – time that would be well spent in visiting the abbey ruins. Return over the green suspension bridge and turn right up the path already used, thus linking back into the return route to Melrose (see below).

To complete the full route, bear left at the abbey entrance on a lane past the toilets to a stile on the left, waymarked as the Border Abbeys Way. It leads to a green track running along the high bank of the River Tweed. After 1.5km, bear slightly left on a track that rises through woodland above a river cliff. The track descends a little and bends left; here take a field gate ahead. Follow the field edge above the river to join a track into more woods. Where this bends left, leave the signed Border Abbeys Way to take a waymarked path down to the right. It joins a road just north of the handsome stone **Mertoun Bridge**.

Cross the bridge and take steps on the right down to the riverbank. ▶ Follow the riverside path round a big left bend, then bear slightly left along the left edge of St

*Eildon North Hill seen from St Cuthbert's Way path above the River Tweed*

From here to the green suspension bridge is waymarked as St Cuthbert's Way.

Boswells golf course. At a tarmac lane turn up left, taking a right turn by a high wall and then bending left into **St Boswells**.

Turn right along the main street, passing shops and bending round to the left. Turn right into Hamilton Place; at its end turn right, then bear left on a path that follows a stream down to the River Tweed.

The riverside path runs along the steep wooded bank with railings, steps and little bridges, before joining a wider track to the green suspension bridge crossed on the outward walk. ◄

*The short-cut from Dryburgh Abbey rejoins the main route here.*

Rejoin the outward route, taking the stepped path ahead onto the high bank of the river. It descends three flights of wooden steps; at the foot of these, turn right on a path that crosses a footbridge then runs alongside the Tweed. After 500 metres, the path turns inland past a signpost for Newton St Boswells. Follow it ahead, to the left of a stream, then rise to a field edge. Take the track ahead, under the A68. It becomes a lane under the disused railway to the B6340 at the north end of Newton St Boswells.

*From here to the walk end is marked as Border Abbeys Way.*

Turn right for 100 metres, then left in a road signed for Eildon village. ◄ This is the disused former A6091, and has the road markings and catseyes to prove it. After 1km (with Eildon village down to the right) pass a barrier closing the road to cars. After another 1km alongside Bogleburn Strip (a belt of trees) pass the site of Thomas the Rhymer's fateful nap.

## TRUE THOMAS

*True Thomas lay on Huntlie Bank*
*Spying ferlies [marvels] wi his eye*
*And there he spied a lady bright*
*Come riding down by Eildon Tree.*
Ballad of True Thomas

She was, of course, the Queen of the Fairies. Thomas woke up seven years later limp and wrung-out, with a smile on his face and outstanding skills in spontaneous verse.

*Melrose Abbey – the heart of Robert the Bruce is buried here*

In another 100 metres pass the second barrier across the road. At once bear right down a hedged track. Where it reaches the A6091, turn down right to pass under the road and the disused railway. Turn left on a wide path, following it ahead and down to a junction at the western end of **Newstead**. ▸

*The Roman fort underneath Newstead justifies its claim as the oldest inhabited village in the UK.*

Turn left in Dean Road. After 50 metres, bear right in a driveway to a fenced path to the left of pony stables. The path runs above a small stream and into a housing estate at the edge of Melrose. Keep ahead along the street, and then onto a tarmac path. This runs alongside **Melrose Abbey**, of which you get fine views free of charge, to emerge in the town centre.

The walk start at the market cross is up to the left.

## THE BORDER ABBEYS

The wealthy and conspicuous Border abbeys were frequent targets for English raids. The campaign that destroyed them was carried out by Henry VIII's general the Earl of Hertford in the 1540s, aimed at persuading the Scots to marry their infant Queen Mary to England's Prince Edward (later King Edward VI).

The war was nicknamed the 'Rough Wooing' by its Scots victims, but was a campaign of destruction and terror that has been compared with the Nazi Blitzkrieg of 1940. Hertford boasted that he had burned down 192 'towns, towers, stedes, barmkyns, parish churches, and castell houses', while driving away into England 10,386 cattle, 12,429 sheep, 1296 horses and 200 goats.

Today a 70 mile (110km) footpath, the Border Abbeys Way, links the four destroyed by Hertford – Melrose, Dryburgh, Kelso and Jedburgh.

# WALK 32
*Rubers Law*

| | |
|---|---|
| **Start/Finish** | Denholm village (NT 567 184) |
| **Distance** | 12km (7½ miles) |
| **Ascent** | 450m (1500ft) |
| **Approx time** | 4hrs |
| **Terrain** | Paths, tracks, grassy field edges |
| **Max altitude** | Rubers Law, 424m |
| **Maps** | Landranger 80 (Cheviot Hills); Explorer 331 (Teviotdale S) |
| **Public transport** | Bus 20 (Hawick–Kelso) |
| **Parking** | Denholm village green |

> *Dark Ruberslaw, that lifts his head sublime,*
> *Rugged and hoary with the wrecks of time;*
> *On his broad misty front the giant wears*
> *The horrid furrows of ten thousand years.*

So wrote John Leyden of Denholm, born in 1775, general peasant prodigy and ballad gatherer for Walter Scott. Leyden was also an early hill-walker, crossing 40 miles to get the last two verses of a ballad and returning at midnight, singing it in his loud, harsh voice.

Denholm is altogether charming, with its wide Georgian green. Denholm Dean is as nice as its name. Rubers Law itself is rocky on top, with a hill fort and a depth of history far exceeding its physical 424m. Here Alexander Peden was almost unique among hill-walkers in wanting mist to come down rather than up. 'Cast the lap of Thy cloak ower auld Sandy and thir poor things,' he prayed as redcoats ringed the hill where he was preaching Protestant fundamentalism some time in the 1680s. From a clear sky, cloud descended onto the hill. The redcoats got lost, and Peden and his congregation escaped among the whin bushes.

Leave the village green at its southern corner (where the main road enters from Hawick). Head south on Westgate at the war memorial, passing toilets and a walking signpost for Denholm Dean. After 200 metres look out for a waymarked kissing gate on the right. Steps lead down into **Denholm Dean** woods.

The path heads upstream, crossing the stream by a footbridge and recrossing by another, up to a path T-junction. Turn right, soon with a ford across the stream. On the following rise, take the main path forking uphill

*Denholm village*

The widely spaced bounding fences suggest this is a former drove road.

to join a wide path along the top edge of the woods, with the stream down left. At the end of the wood the path continues as a grass track between fences. ◀ The track runs southwest to end at a lane.

Turn left, going uphill then down to a plantation. At a lane junction, turn right, signed 'Bonchester Bridge'. After 500 metres uphill, take a track down left opposite **Whitriggs farm**.

The track dips to cross Dean Burn, then runs uphill, entering a stream slot. At the gate at its top, turn right through another gate, and go up a field edge to the right of the plantation. At a corner of the plantation, head uphill and slightly left to a narrow gate in a stone wall.

With a higher plantation over on your left, head up to a gate at the large field's top left corner. Keep uphill beside the fence, through another gate, to the ridgeline wall. Here turn left through a gate, and take a path slightly downhill to the col south of Rubers Law. Fork right on a path zigzagging up the end of the hill fort, among dark

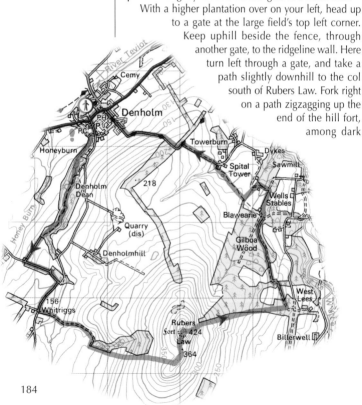

184

dolerite outcrops, to the trig point on the **Rubers Law** summit. ▸

Descend steeply east to a small gate at a bottom corner of the wall below. A small path leads down to a clump of conifers not far below, at the top of a recently felled plantation.

Head downhill to the right of a wall on a grassy path that descends into a little dry valley. At its foot, bear down left to a gate into the woods on the left. At once take a downhill track near the plantation edge to reach a T-junction just above the Rule valley road.

The road is just down to the right through a vehicle barrier, but instead turn left, gently uphill. The track passes across an open field, turns uphill in a woodland strip, then crosses a second field. It runs gently downhill in attractive **Gilboa Wood** to a junction below **Blawearie** houses.

Turn up towards the houses, but just before them, take a rough track on the right into woods. Keep along the top edge of the open woodland until a stile on the left leads into a field corner. This has a Border Abbeys Way marker, and the route follows these waymarks back to Denholm. ▸

Locally the hill name is written as one word, Ruberslaw.

Note that for the next mile, the Border Abbeys Way does not follow the line marked for it on maps.

*On Rubers Law, looking east towards The Cheviot*

*Minto Law, Minto Craigs and Fatlips Castle from track above Denholm*

Cross the stile and bend to the right around the plantation edge. Just before Heathfield Cottage, a waymark points out to the left. Cross an open field southwest, keeping ahead with the field edge wall on your right. With a wood corner just ahead, turn right across a stile and gate with a tall waymark post. Head across the open field northwest to pass a waymark post and head down beyond it to a gate with stile. Just down ahead, join the corner of a gravel track.

It leads down to **Spital Tower** (no tower, just a farm); here turn left over an old bridge onto an uphill track. At its top, turn up left, signposted for Denholm. In 50 metres turn right into the wood, at the top of a stony surfaced path. This runs downhill between hedges.

Across the Teviot valley, on top of the wooded Minto Craigs, is visible the ruined tower of **Fatlips Castle**. Fatlips himself was the head of a small but vicious Border clan, the Turnbulls of Bedrule.

The path turns right to descend into **Denholm**. At the main A698, turn left to the village green.

# 5 LOTHIAN

*Sunrise over Dunbar, from the coast near North Berwick Law (Walk 38)*

# INTRODUCTION

*Evening view from Salisbury Crags to Edinburgh Castle (Walk 34)*

The land of the hill fringes leads gently down into Edinburgh. Lothian is another ancient kingdom – it takes its name from King Lot, who was father-in-law to King Arthur. Latterly it was split into West, Mid and East Lothians, only to reassemble briefly as a local government region between 1975 and 1994.

For a place that doesn't actually exist any more, it's well equipped with hills. Two substantial chunks of the Southern Uplands edge up to form its southern boundary. And as that north edge of the hills is a well-marked fault line, there are great views northwards to the Forth during the ascent onto the Lammermuirs (Walk 36) or the Moorfoots (Walk 35).

Strictly, the Southern Uplands stop there. But the hills continue, with the steep-sided Pentlands (Walk 33) rising excitingly out of the so-called Scottish Lowlands. Meanwhile, one of the UK's finest mini-mountains stands in the centre of Edinburgh itself, Arthur's Seat (Walk 34), and another rises enticingly above the shoreline as North Berwick Law (Walk 38).

# WALK 33
*Pentlands*

| | |
|---|---|
| **Start/Finish** | Flotterstone (NT 232 630) |
| **Distance** | 25km (15½ miles) |
| **Ascent** | 1100m (3700ft) |
| **Approx time** | 9hrs |
| **Terrain** | Good paths, small tracks and tarred lane |
| **Max altitude** | Scald Law, 579m |
| **Maps** | Landranger 66 (Edinburgh); Explorer 344 (Pentland Hills); Harveys Pentland Hills |
| **Public transport** | Bus 101/102 from Edinburgh; this also allows linear walks, such as from Carlops to Fairmilehead |
| **Parking** | Flotterstone Inn. Car park (can fill up on Sundays) 100 metres in from the main road. Alternative car parks Castlelaw or Hillend (below Caerketton). |
| **Variant** | Short-cut back by Glencorse lane – 15.5km (9½ miles) with 750m (2500ft) of ascent (about 5½hrs) |

The Pentlands, rising at Edinburgh's back door, are pathed and popular. And rightly so – the ridgeline from Turnhouse Hill to the Kips is as fine a bit of ridgewalking as any in the Southern Uplands – although technically their pinkish volcanic rocks belong to the Central Belt or Lowlands. At the northern end of the walk, Allermuir and Caerketton have vast views over Edinburgh and the Firth of Forth.

Paths are well used and well maintained by the Pentland Hills Regional Park. The smooth paths and the faint illumination from Edinburgh's streetlights make this an enjoyable place for night-time walks as well.

To the left of the visitor centre, take a path through woods. It passes under trees alongside the lane into Glencorse, then rejoins it. In another 50 metres, turn left through a gate signed 'Scald Law' onto a wide path. Bear left over a footbridge, then bear right to reach the broad path up the end of Turnhouse Hill. The path then runs on the left flank to reach the central cairn of **Turnhouse Hill**.

*On Scald Law, towards East Kip and West Kip*

The wide ridge path descends southwest, dips to a slight rise, then dips into a deep col, with gate and stile. The path is now quite steep, but repaired, to the sprawling Stone Age cairn on **Carnethy Hill**. A wide ridge path leads down west-southwest to a levelling, then a col below. After another gate with stile, zigzag up the repaired steep path to the trig point on **Scald Law**.

Gask Hill 412

Bowler's By

Hare Hill 449

The Howe

Lo Re

Waterfalls

Pentland Hills Regional Park

Red Gate

Logan Burn

Scald Law 579

534

West Kip 551

East Kip

18

19 563 South Black Hill

Eastside

Cap Law

Head down southwest, with the path not all that clear. As the ridgeline flattens, ignore a path bearing left

along the level ridge, but fork down right on the main path, which is clear and eroded, down to a col. Keep ahead steeply up **East Kip** and along the ridge to the slightly rocky **West Kip**. The path leads down southwest to a multiple path junction in a col. Turn right, signposted for Balerno, on a track that bends right to the right of a plantation, then crosses a stream by a stone bridge. At the ridgeline ahead a wall crosses, but 50 metres

*West Kip*

Hare Hill could be crossed from here, but the northeast end is boggy with heather. Black Hill, as the name implies, is heathery as well, hence avoided on this route.

before this turn right on a green track. It contours northeast along the side of **Hare Hill**. ◄

With the deep drop before Black Hill ahead, the green track turns downhill, right, to a fence, then sharp back left to slant down into the steep-sided glen. Turn right on a wide path, passing below a waterfall, then go through a mildly rocky defile for 400 metres to cross a footbridge. Head downvalley to the right of the stream to **The Howe** house. In front of it, recross the stream on a smooth track. The track becomes a tarred lane past two **reservoirs**.

### Short-cut by Glencorse lane

With a substantial slice of Pentland hill-walking already done, there's a quick exit at this point. The lane ahead bends round along the eastern side of **Glencorse Reservoir**, leading back to Flotterstone after 2km.

This short-cut can equally be used in the opposite direction. Coming in up the valley-floor lane from the car park to this point leads into an outing over the Edinburgh end of the range. The route continues, as described below, over Capelaw Hill, Allermuir and Castlelaw, giving 11.5km (7 miles) with 350m (1200ft) of ascent (about 3½hrs).

## PHYSICS IN THE HILLS

Charles TR Wilson, born nearby and commemorated by a pathside plaque, was the first Nobel prizewinner inspired by Scottish mountains. It was on ascents of Ben Nevis to its observatory that he invented the Cloud Chamber, an ingenious device for generating visible condensation trails along the pathways of cosmic rays and other subatomic particles. (And the second? Edinburgh hill-walker Professor Peter Higgs got his in 2014 for the Higgs Boson notion he came up with when walking in the Cairngorms.)

Just past the track end of **Kirkton farm**, cross a stream and turn up left off the lane on a wide path signed for Balerno and Colinton. Head up beside a wood for 400 metres, then turn right signed 'Colinton'.

Follow the wide path, somewhat torn about by mountain bikes, around the flank of **Harbour Hill** (ignoring an ancient range warning sign), through a gate, and up to the path's highest point. Turn right at cross paths up **Capelaw Hill**.

From the main top, the path heads down quite steeply to a gate and stile. Fork up left to meet a gritty military track. Go straight across it on a path to the summit of **Allermuir Hill**. The 1km (each way) to Caerketton Hill is a pleasant ridge walk with views across Edinburgh to the Forth and Fife. A wide path runs to the left of a fence all the way to **Caerketton** summit. Return to **Allermuir Hill**.

Retrace steps briefly along the fence, then follow it down the ridgeline south to join the military track in a col. The track skirts left of **Castlelaw Hill**. Just above Castlelaw farm, divert right to visit the souterrain within **Castlelaw Hill Fort**.

The **souterrain**, or earth house – an underground chamber within the earthworks – has been opened up for the modern visitor, quite literally, with a doubling of the passageway height and glass roof lights. Only the crawl through the low arch into the inner chamber gives the authentic crouched-in-puddle underground experience.

From the fort, head straight down to the track foot into **Castlelaw farm**. Pass through the small car park. A fenced path with signpost leads around below the farm to join a dirt track beyond. Follow this for 400 metres until a signpost points down left for Flotterstone. The path runs down to join the Glencorse lane. Turn left along it to Flotterstone.

# WALK 34

*Arthur's Seat*

| | |
|---|---|
| **Start/Finish** | St Margaret's Loch (NT 277 740) |
| **Distance** | 4km (2½ miles) |
| **Ascent** | 300m (1000ft) |
| **Approx time** | 1½hrs |
| **Terrain** | Paths, some steep and rough |
| **Max altitude** | Arthur's Seat, 251m |
| **Maps** | Landranger 66 (Edinburgh); Explorer 350 (Edinburgh); Harveys Edinburgh Seven Hills |
| **Public transport** | Frequent buses from Edinburgh city centre to Meadowbank; or walk from Holyrood House at the foot of the Royal Mile |
| **Parking** | Car park off the Duke's Walk |

The rockiest hilltop between Lakeland and Loch Lomond lies within the city limits of Edinburgh. A century ago, one Scottish climber stood with his Alpine guide and asked, 'How long to climb it?' The guide looked hard at the basalt crags. 'A strong party could do it in a day.'

Okay, Arthur's Seat isn't as big as it looks. From the summit, on a clear day, you can still hear the bagpiper in Princes Street. As mountains go this is an extremely small one. So this leaves plenty of time to take the open-top bus tour and explore the souvenir shops of the Royal Mile.

From the car park, take a path southwest past a notice-board, with St Anthony's Chapel seen up ahead. Cross

the end of Queen's Drive to swan-infested St Margaret's Loch. Pass along the left side, below **St Anthony's Chapel** ruin. At the loch end keep ahead through the low col to the left of the rocky knoll Haggis Knowe.

Keep ahead (west) across the foot of Hunters Bog valley and up a steepening slope to the top of the north end of **Salisbury Crags**. ▶ Follow the crag brink all the way along, with views over the city. Eventually the crag dwindles to its end at the col (109m) at the head of Hunters Bog.

Here walkers can turn back right, below the crag, for 50 metres to admire Hutton's Section. Scramble the low crag above and retrace your previous steps to the col.

Cross the col to a steep and eroded-looking gully (the Hawse) up the face of Arthur's Seat. A stone pitched path zigzags up between two lumpy basalt crags – the one to the left being the Gutted Haddie (haddock). At the gully head the path slants out to the right and contours

*Arthur's Seat, seen over Edinburgh, from the castle*

The view down is onto Holyrood Palace – you can watch the Queen's garden parties from here.

195

## ARTHUR'S SEAT GEOLOGY

Salisbury Crag is a classic example of a dolerite sill – molten rock squeezed out between other strata. Quarrying has emphasised it. At nearby Hutton's Section an interpretation board explains how James Hutton, Scotland's first geologist, here came to an understanding of the origin of the rocks. The dolerite did not crystallise out of the oceans of Noah's Flood. Behind the noticeboard it can be seen how a raft of sedimentary sandstone has been swept up into the dolerite, which must (accordingly) have been a molten liquid mass.

Arthur's Seat, as a geology field trip, could take a full day in itself. To the left of Hutton's Section, sandstone can be seen below the dolerite sill with a heat-treated upper edge, again displaying the molten nature of the dolerite. Scramble above the noticeboard to see that the rock has small gas-bubble holes or 'vesicles'.

Arthur's Seat summit is volcanic agglomerate, a welded lumpy mass from the vent of the former volcano. To the east, the Lang Rig is not another dolerite sill but a lava flow that formed in the open air. And to the west of Hunter's Bog, Camstane Quarries show sandstone with fossilised ripples of the former sea bed, and also polygonal cracks from what was once sun-dried mud.

around the south end of Nether Hill – views now are south to the Pentlands. The path turns up left to cross Nether Hill's grassy summit, drops slightly, and then tackles the bare, footworn rocks of **Arthur's Seat** summit.

From the viewpoint indicator, your descent is just north of east. Pass to the left of the trig point and descend the bare rock spur. Ahead and below is a loch which shouldn't be confused with St Margaret's Loch, where you started off. It is in fact **Dunsapie Loch**; aim towards its right-hand end on a path zigzagging between erosion-control fences. At a slight hill shoulder, take a path back sharply left, slanting down across the steep face of Arthur's Seat above the head of the valley called the Dry Dam.

Once across the steepest slope, fork right on the path running down into the Dry Dam. Follow the valley down (it is, in fact, a tiny hanging valley). Just before its end, fork right to the ruin of **St Anthony's Chapel**. Here turn down right on a fairly steep path to St Margaret's Loch.

# WALK 35

*Blackhope Scar*

| | |
|---|---|
| **Start/Finish** | Gladhouse Reservoir (NT 288 535) |
| **Alternative** | |
| **Start/Finish** | (with parking) Near road junction at northeast corner of reservoir (NT 309 541) or off-road parking area on Moorfoot lane (NT 291 528) |
| **Distance** | 23.5km (14½ miles) |
| **Ascent** | 500m (1700ft) |
| **Approx time** | 6½hrs |
| **Terrain** | Hill paths; 2km of very rough moorland; tracks and road |
| **Max altitude** | Blackhope Scar, 651m |
| **Maps** | Landranger 73 (Peebles); Explorers 345 (Lammermuir Hills) and 337 (Peebles) |
| **Parking** | Small lay-by west of the reservoir |

Blackhope Scar is the high point of the northern Moorfoots. The foots in question have spent a long time inside the moorland socks, and the summit of Blackhope is a nasty wilderness of heathery peat and old fence wire. But this walk shows that there is more to the Moorfoots – the grassy northern slope offers views across Gladhouse Reservoir to the Pentlands and the sea, and the walk explores the hidden valleys of Blackhope Water and the River South Esk.

Head north to the nearby junction, and turn right towards **Gladhouse**. After 200 metres, a stile provides access to the reservoir side and a small path that leads under pines to the reservoir dam end. Cross it, and the bridge beyond, to continue along the lane – there's another short diversion off the road and along the shoreline between two defunct car parks.

Turn right towards **Mauldslie** at the reservoir's northeast corner. ▶ At the lane end, with the farm on your right, keep ahead on a green track marked for Heriot and Blackhope.

Alternative start/finish

The track runs to the
left of Roddy Cleugh to
a gate, where it fades
at the start of moor-
land of grass and
rushes. Head out
into the moor

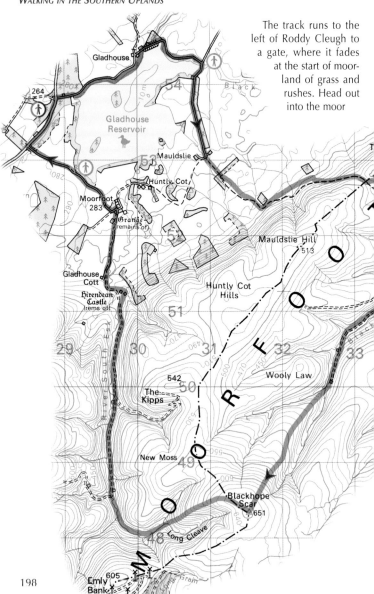

southeast. With luck, in 200 metres a lone waymark post is passed, where a faint path starts. It crosses a stile to meet a clearer path at the foot of the steeper slope that marks the edge of the Southern Uplands. (An area of cleared plantation is just below.)

Turn left along the path, still following the slope foot. Cross a stream (Wesley Cleugh Burn) and in another 400 metres arrive above another clear-felled plantation. Here turn directly uphill, for a rough 150 metres, to find the small old path marked on maps.

This grassy little path slants uphill, with widening views across Lothian to the Pentlands, then curves up into a wide pass. Through the gate here, turn up left (waymark post) with a fence on your left. Another post marks the start of a grassy track just down to the right of the nondescript **Torfichen Hill South** (468m).

The clear green track runs down just south of east towards a hill road. Before reaching this another track, made of black

*Blackhope Scar from Torfichen Hill*

gravel, becomes visible just below. Head down to join this and turn right, away from the road.

The track runs up the valley of Blackhope Water. Keep to the left of **Blackhope farm**, going upstream another 1.5km to sheepfolds. Here the track fords the stream; stay on the same side briefly to find a bridge opposite a grouse-shooter's hut (often open).

*The spur is named Glowrin' Lee on Explorer maps.*

Beyond the hut, continue upstream on a grassy track for 500 metres to another hut. Just beyond it, the track ends at a rough bridge. Cross this, and head up the spur above. ◄

The spur-line is grassy heather, and a reasonable line up can be found by keeping to its left edge, above Blackhope Water. The slope becomes rough grassland as it steepens, but the summit plateau is rough peat and heather for the final struggle to the trig point on **Blackhope Scar**.

*The hidden approach to Blackhope Scar along Blackhope Water*

The summit gives a brief taste of the plateau ground of **the Moorfoots** – considered by many as the nastiest in the Southern Uplands with its mixture of peat, black puddles and dark heather.

Follow the fence line down northwest for 400 metres to its slight bend right. Then, with relief, veer off left onto the spur of Cleave Rig. This leads down to the stream junction of Little Cleave and **Long Cleave**, at the very head of the **River South Esk**. Continue downstream on grassy banks. At a brick shepherd's shed a track arrives from up on the left and leads on comfortably downvalley past a second shed.

*Hirendean Castle, to the Pentlands*

A gate marks the exit from the valley. Here a small path slants up ahead towards what looks like a bent cairn, but is in fact the tip of the ruined **Hirendean Castle**, a 16th-century pele tower poised at the very edge of the Southern Uplands. From the castle, head downhill to rejoin the track as it crosses the South Esk. It leads on northwards to **Moorfoot farm**.

Turn left among the buildings to the start of the tarmac road, which runs past the corner of **Gladhouse Reservoir**. ▶ Follow the road to a T-junction with a wider road. Turn right for 500 metres to the walk start.

*Alternative start/finish*

# WALK 36
## *Lammer Law*

| | |
|---|---|
| **Start/Finish** | Old Lauder Road above Longyester (NT 538 637) |
| **Alternative Start/Finish** | (with parking) Road end below Hopes Reservoir (NT 557 633) |
| **Distance** | 14km (9 miles) |
| **Ascent** | 400m (1300ft) |
| **Approx time** | 4½hrs |
| **Terrain** | Tracks and path; finish by small roads or by field edges and grass moor |
| **Max altitude** | Lammer Law, 527mm |
| **Maps** | Landranger 66 (Edinburgh); Explorer 345 (Lammermuirs) – note 5m contour interval, making slopes look extra steep |
| **Access** | Occasionally between 12th August and November there may be grouse shooting. It would not normally affect walkers on this route, who will be sticking to the moorland tracks. |
| **Parking** | Verge parking at gate onto open hill at end of tarred road; also at track end in Blinkbonny Wood (NT 542 643) |
| **Variants** | Short-cut to Lammer Law (neglible differences); road finish – adds 1.5km (1 mile) (about ¼hr) |

Lucy of Lammermuir (in Walter Scott's novel), who became Lucia (in Donizetti's opera), went slowly mad while breaking all the castle windows with her top F. And it's true the Lammermuirs can be a little oppressive, with their calf-deep heather, their black peat, and their endless gently rolling moors. However, since Lucy's time they've been considerably tamed with Landrover tracks, and these days a windfarm twinkles from almost every top.

The highest Lammermuir is Meikle Says Law, but Lammer Law, which names the whole range, is a better hill. A handy old road leads right past its summit, and that summit has wide views northwards to the Forth, as well as an ancient cairn.

Through a gate, the tarmac road continues as a clear track (the Old Lauder Road) heading up roughly south-west onto Threep Law, which is the northeast ridge of Lammer Law. At 450m a fence approaches from down on the left; opposite the fence corner a faint wheelmark track forks off right.

**Short-cut to Lammer Law**
This track runs directly to Lammer Law, but becomes very faint on the heathery moorland. It could be followed – running above and parallel with the main track for a while, then bending up right across the moorland crest. It leads to a gate in a crossing fence. Cross a stony track running behind the fence, as the fainter green track runs ahead for the last 200 metres to the cairn of **Lammer Law**.

The main track continues up the left flank of Threep Law, passing through a gate. In another 300 metres look out for a small gate up on the right. Through it, a peaty path runs to the left of a fence. After 250 metres it meets a stony track. The cairn of

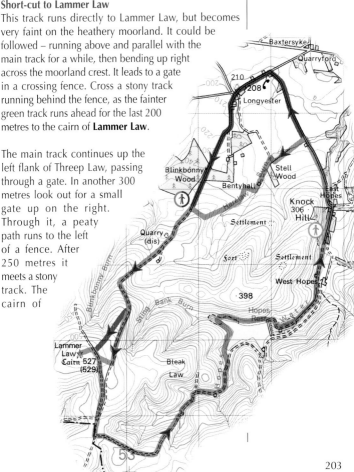

Lammer Law is now seen ahead across the heather, but turn right, along the track, for 150 metres, then left on a grassy track to **Lammer Law** summit, with its large ancient cairn.

Return to the stony track and turn right (south) as it runs down the moorland crest towards a major col. Just above the col, the Old Lauder Road rejoins from the left. In the col itself, a metal gate is ahead, but turn left in front of it through a wooden one. A track leads gently downhill, along the rim of the Harley Grain hollow that runs down towards Hopes Reservoir. After 1km the track bends left and descends into the stream hollow.

The track winds its way down the stream hollow to a ford, with a corner of Hopes Reservoir visible ahead. Here bear left on a grassy quad-bike path. It recrosses the stream and continues beside it, then slants up to the left to run above the fence surrounding the **Hopes Reservoir**.

The path works around one reservoir peninsula, then descends steeply to the **Sting Bank Burn** at the reservoir's northwest corner. Head up beside the fence to a gate at its top corner. Now a small path runs through birch woods along the steep slope above the reservoir.

*On the north slope of Lammer Law*

*Small path running above Hopes Reservoir*

After 800 metres, a stile down on the right leads to the north end of the **dam**. Just to the left, a stony track winds down under the trees, then runs out along the valley floor below the dam. It passes down to the left of **West Hopes.** ▶ In another 1km the track crosses a cattle grid to the start of the tarmac road at the water-filtering plant. There's a parking area on the right here. ▶

Follow the quiet road downvalley. It crosses Hopes Water at **East Hopes**, rises across a spur of Knock Hill, and descends to cross **Harelaw Burn**.

The Explorer map confidently marks the line of the Old Lauder Road here. It is not visible on the ground, and following its line involves pathless field edges and fence climbing.

### Alternative route – road via Longyester

The simpler alternative follows the road on towards Longyester. After another 1km turn left at a T-junction, signposted for **Longyester**. There is (until BT removes it) a phone box here and a few parking spaces. After 500 metres pass Longyester farm and turn left up the dead-end road, with a road signpost for Lammer Law. Follow this back to the start.

To follow the non-existent former road, just after the bridge take a field gate on the left. Follow the left edge of the field to the right of the stream. At its end, cross

The farmhouse mixes grey Southern Upland slate with orange east-coast pantiles.

Alternative start/finish

205

the stream and pass along to the left of a strip of recently felled woodland.

At the field end, a gate on the right leads to a track across the former plantation. Turn left, roughly southwest, past a corner of **Stell Wood** and then along a line of tall old beeches. ◄ Continue, with a fence on your left, to reach a field corner alongside Harelaw Burn.

The beeches are probably the hedge that ran alongside the former road.

One option is to cross the awkward fence corner onto the open moorland, and turn up right to a wall. Alternatively, if the fence is just too awkward, head up it for 200 metres to a gate, then back down the fence to the same wall. Head along the moorland edge to the left of the wall, passing through a gate in a crossing fence. Ignore a first gate on the right, but immediately beyond the corner of the wall turn right through a second gate. A short track leads to the foot of the hill track onto Lammer Law.

# WALK 37
*Abbey St Bathans and Cockburn Law*

| | |
|---|---|
| Start/Finish | Edin's Hall Broch car park just off A6112 north of Preston (NT 788 609) |
| Alternative Start/Finish | (with parking) Abbey St Bathans (NT 763 618) |
| Distance | 12.5km (8 miles) |
| Ascent | 350m (1100ft) |
| Approx time | 4hrs |
| Terrain | Tracks, path, and 800 metres of field edge |
| Max altitude | Cockburn Law, 325m |
| Maps | Landranger 67 (Duns); Explorer 345 (Lammermuirs) – note 5m contour interval, making slopes look extra steep |
| Parking | Small car park at wood corner, signposted from A6112 for Edin's Hall Broch |

Abbey St Bathans is a village almost invisible among the hidden curves of the Whiteadder Water. But over the last couple of millennia a few strangers have managed to find the place – from the gruesome giant Edin, who imprisoned a wife here, to Irish monk St Bathan and the Ghurkas who built the handsome footbridge halfway around the walk.

The hill part of this walk is Cockburn Law, a mere 325m high. But the strange Edin's Hall Broch (circular tower), below it, is a big one! The rest of the way is riverside and a woodland track.

Just below the car park pull-in, a track signed for Edin's Hall Broch runs down to the left into the woods. Ignore a track forking up right (the return route) and follow the main track down to the Whiteadder Water.

A sign points left to the nearby footbridge hidden in foliage. It crosses a rocky corner of the river to **Elba** cottage. ▶ Turn right in front of the cottage on a path that runs through woods to emerge into a long field alongside the river.

Nothing to do with Napoleon – the cottage sits above the 'Elba' of the river.

Follow the right edge of the field, next to the river, then turn up left alongside a wall to a stile with a green signboard, again marking the way to Edin's Hall. The path runs along above a fence, then a wall, with another stile and then a kissing gate onto open hill.

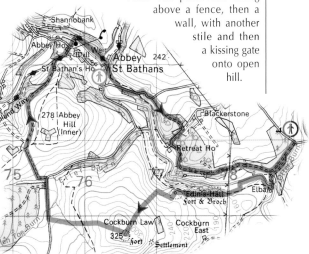

*Edin's Hall Broch to Whiteadder Water*

The path divides, but the way is slanting up the hill slope ahead to its crest, with the low stone walls which are the remains of **Edin's Hall**.

Immediately above the broch, a fence across the hillside has a stile in it. Across the stile turn right on a path across a downhill corner of the field to a stile and signpost.

Turn uphill for Cockburn Law. What path there is was formed by hooves as much as by boots. However,

### EDIN'S HALL – BROCH OR WHAT?

At the corner of some humpy remains of a prehistoric fortified settlement rises this odd structure. A broch is a circular stone tower, built some time in the Iron Age. It has a narrow entrance tunnel, with guard chambers in the walls on either side. It has other small rooms built into the thickness of the walls, as well as a staircase leading to the top of the rampart. Edin's Hall seems to be a broch.

Then again, brochs were built, it is thought, for defence against Norsemen. They are found on the coast of Wester Ross and on the Hebridean islands. Edin's Hall is in the Lowlands, and a long way inland. It is also about twice as wide as the other brochs.

So it's not a broch at all, but was built as a summerhouse and prison by three-headed giant Red Edin, who seized the King of Scotland's daughter and installed her on this lonely hillside. While waiting for her rescue by the third son of a widow, she will have had a chance to enjoy the fine view down onto the wooded Whiteadder valley.

the slope is mostly grassy. Move about 100 metres to the left on the way up to avoid the main bracken patch. Cross rings of fortification to the **Cockburn Law** trig point.

Head down a vague ridgeline of rough grass, roughly northwest, aiming towards the corner of Hen Toe Wood in the valley below. Fences from either side converge on a pair of gates. Take the one on the left to head down the left-hand edge of a field westwards. Cross a stream ditch and rise slightly to the field corner at a hill road.

Turn right and head down the road to a bend at the valley floor. Here turn off left on a rough tractor track. It runs west for 100 metres, then turns right, up the field edge, to a gate at a col west of **Abbey Hill (Inner)**. An earthwork just to the left is currently used to store silage in black bags.

Through the gate take a track to the right, but in a few steps bear left. A clear tractor track runs roughly north, around the slope of Abbey Hill (Inner), passing through two gates to reach the top edge of Mountjoy Wood. The track runs down along the wood's top, then more steeply. The SU Way joins from the left, and the combined track runs down between walls to the road at **Abbey St Bathans**.

*The Ghurka Bridge at Abbey St Bathans*

Cross to a track past the church (Lammermuir Kirk) and a long footbridge, the Ghurka Bridge. Over this, turn right on a wide path through woods alongside the river. After 600 metres this crosses a small footbridge to a sign-post. Here the SU Way turns away to the left, and another long footbridge on the right would lead across to Abbey St Bathans village car park and small café. ◀ But take the wooded path ahead, signposted as a public footpath.

*Alternative start/finish*

The path slants up through woods, then across scrubby grassland above the river, to reach a track. Turn left, signed 'Public footpath'. Follow the track up through the wood to its top, then turn right on a track along the wood top. This descends to meet a tarmac lane.

Turn right, downhill, and just above the **Retreat House** mansion bend left over a stone bridge. The track passes above the house and into woods. Keep ahead on the main track, with the river occasionally seen down on your right. After almost 2km join the track of the outward route, keeping ahead for the final 500 metres to the parking pull-off.

# WALK 38
## *North Berwick Law*

| | |
|---|---|
| **Start/Finish** | Aberlady Bay (NT 471 804) |
| **Distance** | 31km (19½ miles) |
| **Ascent** | 300m (1000ft) |
| **Approx time** | 8hrs |
| **Terrain** | Field tracks; 3.5km quiet roads; hill path and rough coastal paths |
| **Max altitude** | North Berwick Law, 187m |
| **Maps** | Landranger 66 (Edinburgh); Explorer 351 (Dunbar) – note 5m contour interval, making slopes look extra steep |
| **Public transport** | Bus X24 (Edinburgh–North Berwick) stops at Aberlady and Gullane |
| **Parking** | Alongside A198 at east end of Aberlady |
| **Variant** | Start at Gullane (NT 477 831) – 24.5km (15½ miles) with 250m (800ft) of ascent (about 6½hrs) |

North Berwick Law is splendidly steep sided and rocky, with sea views right up into the Highlands. It is often walked as a fine short outing from North Berwick (taking in the harbour, Plattcock End and The Glen in a circuit of about 4.5km). However, a hill so handsome and so dominant above East Lothian deserves to be treated as if it were a big day out. On this walk, this is achieved simply by starting quite a long way away, at Aberlady, which adds to the expedition a long stretch of sand dunes and sea-buckthorn shrubbery – astonishingly wild for somewhere only 20 miles from Edinburgh.

A John Muir Way signpost points east along the pavement of the A198. ▶ After 800 metres, turn off right, signposted for Luffness Mains, and at once turn left in a smaller road signed for Kingston. Optionally, use the field edge to the right of the road, heading to a driveway on the right towards The Kennels.

The John Muir Way was extended in 2014 to Helensburgh on the Clyde.

Where the track bends right to a house keep ahead into woods on a track called Dreem Ride. Across a reservoir on the left there is a first, very distant view of North Berwick Law. In open field the track bends left to a complex junction. At the track T-junction turn right for 100 metres, then left to another T-junction near horse huts. Here turn right on a concrete track.

After 1.2km the track bends left beside a road. Turn right in woods beside the road to find a hedge gap, where it's possible to cross onto the road itself. ▶ Take the track opposite, marked to '2nd Time Around', a shed selling old furniture.

A lay-by (possible parking spot) is immediately on the right.

map continues on page 212

The grassy track continues east for 800 metres, then turns north to **East Fenton farm**. Turn right to pass the farm buildings. Where the tarmac driveway turns up left keep ahead past a row of handsome cottages, then turn left on a farm track. ◀ In the

The pink-rendered Fenton Tower is over on the right.

second field this turns left, but keep ahead along a ditch. At a fence corner turn left, around an abandoned **quarry**, to join the access track to a composting facility. Turn right along this to a minor road.

Turn right for what will be 3.5km of road. (The shorter route from Gullane joins here.) The lane passes over a railway and ahead through **Kingston** onto the B1347. Where this bends left, keep ahead on a smaller road for 800 metres. The lane jinks left, and where it bends back right again, there's a kissing gate ahead with John Muir Way signpost.

map continues on page 214

North Berwick Law, directly ahead now, is one of the **Paps of Lothian** – the other being Arthur's Seat. Both are the plugs of Carboniferous volcanoes standing proud above the softer sandstone surroundings. The low ridge running to the right is the 'tail' of the crag-and-tail formation (a rock hill and tapering ridge); it shows that the glacier that scraped the hill into its present shape was moving from west to east.

The path runs along field edges, crossing a tarmac track and continuing as a rough track. After taking a gate and stile on the right, pass down to the left of a muddy pond to a John Muir Way signpost on a track running along the base of North Berwick Law.

Cross the main track and bear right on a path that wanders along the base of the quarried rock face. At its end, the path turns up left to meet the wide, official path up North Berwick Law. This runs up to the right briefly, then zigzags back left to slant around onto the south-west spur of the hill. From here walkers can either head directly uphill, for some gentle scrambling on lumps of dolerite rock, or follow the wide path as it zigzags between. The summit of **North Berwick Law** has a trig point and a viewpoint indicator, as well as a ruined hut and a whale's jawbone arch.

The view from **North Berwick Law** is very wide, extending (according to the viewpoint table) to Glas Maol in the eastern Grampians. More commonly you can see the Forth bridges and across the sea to the Paps of Fife, more respectably known as East and West Lomond.

*On North Berwick Law, looking towards North Berwick, the Firth of Forth and Fife*

The ruin is a military lookout, used in the Napoleonic and also the Second World War. The whalebone arch celebrates North Berwick's proud history as a whaling port, although historians doubt that the port does actually have any such history... The arch rotted away, alas, in 2005, and was replaced with a fibreglass replica.

*Any direct descent towards North Berwick leads over cliffs.*

Return down the southwest spur to a bench on a levelling. ◄ Here either turn down left on the main path's gentle zig-zags or take a direct descent to the right of the bench. Turn right on a wide earth path to the car park below the hill. ◄

*John Muir Way signs will now lead through North Berwick.*

A path beside the access lane leads forward into **North Berwick**. Take the first street on the right, Lochbridge Road, for 200 metres, then turn left on a dirt track that becomes a tarmac path through a little wood. Keep down ahead to cross the A198 into Lodge Grounds. ◄

*A John Muir Way signpost is absent here, but the interpretation board shows its line through the park.*

A few steps into the park, fork left to pass between a playground (left) and a yew arch (right), winding downhill to a gate into the centre of the town. Keep ahead down Quality Street, ignoring (for now) the John Muir Way turning left into High Street, to reach the harbour and a path to the tip of a rocky point (called Plattcock End) beyond.

Return into the town and turn right along High Street. In 300 metres turn right down Church Road for a path that wanders left along grass next to **North Berwick Bay**. At the back left corner, pass around the back of the golf clubhouse and bear right along Pointgarry Road. It passes along the side of the golf course.

*map continues on page 217*

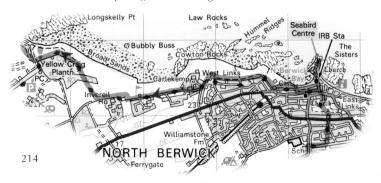

Keep ahead along the edge of the golf course, on a track at first, with a high wall on your left. After a wall gate, the path turns left, then turns right again between walls to a street end.

Turn left to a junction, and here turn right along Abbotsford Road. Soon it has the golf course alongside on its right. At its end, turn right in a fenced path, which bends left and runs alongside the golf course, with the high wall of **Invereil House** on its left.

At the golf-course corner is a gate and signpost. Bear right on a path across open grass and into a wood. At the wood end, the path turns left. It runs with a broken wall and scrubby trees on its left, passing a concrete toilet block, to a track. Here your walk leaves the John Muir Way, which turns left.

Turn right, and in a few metres fork left onto a grassy path to the right-hand corner of **Yellow Craig Plantation**. The path leads around its edge, bending left, onto shoreline with scrubby sea buckthorn on the left. ▶

Offshore is the dolerite Fidra island, with lighthouse; the island has a narrow sea arch on its coast.

## SEA BUCKTHORN

The coastal part of the walk passes over sand and coarse marram grass, through a distinctive ecosystem dominated by sea buckthorn. This thorny shrub is supremely adapted to life in pure sand, with the salty winds off the sea having a drying effect otherwise only found far inland – most of the world's sea buckthorn actually grows in dry deserts around the Himalaya.

*Sea buckthorn, Gullane Bents*

The extended root system helps stabilise the dune. With the sand lacking soil nutrients, the roots also harbour symbiotic bacteria that extract nitrogen from the air. The flowers are unimpressive, and the glory of the bush is in its lurid orange berries, seen from December to February. In late autumn there are still a few drooping yellow leaves to augment the strange colour scheme.

A brief section of the path will be underwater at the highest tides.

The path continues along the shoreline for 1.5km, then descends to the beach. ◄ Pass along the shoreline below two crags, with a **cave** up a short path on the left. The shoreline now turns to grassy sand dunes with awkward sandy paths (or walkers can just stay on the beach).

At a cairn, a wider path turns southwest, across the dunes, to rejoin the coastline beyond the grassy point **Eyebroughy**. Narrow paths run through the dunes (again the beach is easier); then a wider path passes around the seaward edge of a plantation

216

to reach the wide sands of **Gullane Bay**. A wide path heads directly up to a car park below **Gullane**. ▶

The shorter alternative route (see below) begins here.

Turn right on a tarred path, passing a toilet block in woodland. The main path descends back to the beach. Bleaching Rocks cannot be passed at beach level if the tide is high; turn up steep sand to find paths above in the scrubland.

From **Gullane Point**, the path descends onto the wide beach of **Gullane Sands**. After 1km, a sign on the beach marks a footpath turning inland through the dunes. At a wider path, bear right to pass the foot of a golf fairway. Just after this is a junction marked 'footpath' in various directions. Bear right (south), passing to the right of an area of sea buckthorn. A marshy pool is on your right, then the path runs under buckthorn scrub. With the estuary ahead, the path turns left to the long wooden footbridge across the estuary of **Mill Burn**. ▶

The historical novelist Nigel Tranter lived near here, and celebrated the bridge as his 'Footbridge to Enchantment'.

### Shorter walk from Gullane

The Gullane start means not quite such a long walk to achieve North Berwick Law. However, it increases the roadwalk-ing on the outward leg from 3.5km to about 6km.

Start at the **Gullane Bay** car park (NT 477 831). Follow the access lane back into Gullane and along

*'Footbridge to Enchantment', Aberlady Bay*

Sandy Loan to the main **A198**. Turn left through Gullane, and follow John Muir Way signs along the A198's pavement. Just after the lodge cottage where the John Muir Way forks off, cross the A198 to a gate.

A grassy track heads southeast. Cross a ditch and bear left on a firmer track. Pass to the right of farm buildings at **Queenstonbank**, keeping ahead on another field track and passing under a wind turbine. In 400 metres, just before another ditch bridge, the track turns left out to the **B1345**.

Turn right for 400 metres, then left into **Fenton Barns**. At once turn left, signed for Kingston. Soon the longer route is joined, heading into Kingston village. Continue following it (see above) to North Berwick Law and back by the coast to Gullane.

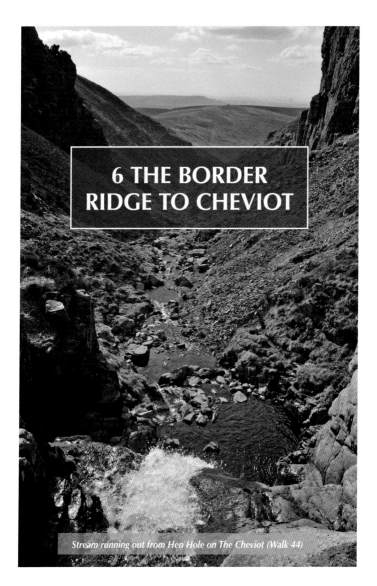

# 6 THE BORDER RIDGE TO CHEVIOT

*Stream running out from Hen Hole on The Cheviot (Walk 44)*

# INTRODUCTION

*Kielder Stane at sunrise (Walk 41)*

Between Liddesdale, at the back of Langholm in the west, and Wooler, in Northumberland, the England–Scotland border forms a long and lonely ridgeline. In over 100km, that ridgeline is crossed by just two motor roads – at the aptly named Deadwater and at Carter Bar.

The pony paths that crossed the bog and heather in the reiving times are grown over and gone. Those paths converged on the Kielder Stone (Walk 41), a gritstone tor right on the border where enemies met in uneasy truce among the midges. The wild lawlessness lingers on, in atmosphere anyway, at unsettling Hermitage Castle below Walk 40.

Across in the east, that border ridgeline is the crest of the hill range called the Cheviots, with The Cheviot itself as their highest point. The Scottish approaches (Walks 42–44) are especially attractive. The foothills are steep sided and grassy, with little twisting valleys in between. Hill forts sit on their tops, and wooded streams and lonely sheep pens lie below.

# WALK 39
## Langholm Heights

| | |
|---|---|
| **Start/Finish** | Langholm, Kiln Green car park (NY 363 848) |
| **Distance** | 15.5km (9½ miles) |
| **Ascent** | 700m (2300ft) |
| **Approx time** | 5¼hrs |
| **Terrain** | Rough grassy ridges, mostly with paths |
| **Max altitude** | Hog Fell, 371m |
| **Maps** | Landranger 79 (Hawick); Explorer 323 (Eskdale) |
| **Public transport** | Bus 95/X95 to Edinburgh and Carlisle, as well as Galashiels and Hawick |
| **Parking** | Kiln Green car park on A7 at north edge of Langholm |
| **Variant** | Return via Potholm farm above River Esk – same distance and time, but more sheltered |

It's tempting to compare this border Eskdale with the South Esk on Walk 35, with the Esks of Yorkshire and Angus, and with the splendid Eskdale in the Lake District. 'Esk' is from Gaelic 'uisge', meaning 'water' or 'river', and valleys do contain rivers rather often! This particular Eskdale makes for green and grassy going, with airy moorlands dropping sharply to a little wood of bluebells. Wrae Hill and Potholm are beautifully carved by their two enfolding rivers.

All around these ridges, the ancient cattle-thieving atmosphere lingers on. The walk overlooks the Tarras Moss, whose bogs and now-vanished thickets were the stronghold of the lawless Armstrongs – their clan museum is at the end of the walk. And the handsome grey town of Langholm preserves this wild heritage in its traditions of horseriding and rugby.

Head downstream past a small play park, then through a hedge gap on the left for a tarmac path up to the main street. Keep ahead, passing the end of the main bridge over the Esk (Telford built it) towards the town hall. Before the town hall, and immediately after the post office, turn left up Kirk Wynd, signed for the golf course. At the lane's top continue up a steep tarred path.

The path keeps relentlessly uphill, passing to the left of the golf course, eventually to emerge through a gate (with stile up right) onto open hill. Here bear up right on a wide path that reaches a stone pyramid beside Whita Well spring with a chained drinking cup. Above is a bench below a small disused quarry in basalt. Take a small steep path up to the left of the quarry, aiming straight for Major Malcolm's stone memorial column. Cross a gravel track just before reaching this tall stone pillar at **Whita Hill** summit.

> The lettering on the pillar is eroding away. But really, could **Major Sir John Malcolm** have been quite so wonderful? 'Probably just like all the rest of them,' suggested one local from the Muckle Toon (Langholm). 'A load of bloody pirates.'

Turn left (north). Either follow the gravel track downhill or take a faint path to the left of the wall for a moorland route that edges down left to rejoin that track. At the track foot, fork off left to visit the iron artwork **memorial** to local poet Hugh Macdiarmid – who would have shared the republican sentiment of his fellow townsman up at the hilltop pillar.

*Hugh Macdiarmid memorial sculpture, Whita Hill*

## HUGH MACDIARMID

The rusty iron monument on Whita Hill commemorates whisky, Scotland's rainfall, curlews, pipe tobacco – and the poet Hugh Macdiarmid. Born in Langholm in 1892, he was a communist and a Scottish Nationalist, and wrote in both English and Lallans (Lowland Scots).

His work includes a fine verse to a fine mountain, Liathach, as well as a translation of Duncan Ban MacIntyre's long verse addressed to another of the Munros, Ben Dorain. His best-known work includes the very long poem 'A Drunk Man Looks at the Thistle'. But for a short one inspired by a patch of soggy moorland – it might well be Hog Fell – look up 'Scotland Small?'

Turn up the hill road to its top. At the crestline wall, turn off left through a gate for a quad-bike path to the left of the wall. Follow this over **Muckle Knowe**, where the wall gives way to a fence. On the descent towards Hog Fell the ground is boggy here and there. The wall restarts on the firmer ground up to the trig point on Hog Fell. ◀ Small outcrops of grey sandstone decorate this summit. Some have bands of quartz pebbles, up to 2cm across, showing that the rock was laid down originally in a stream bed.

Note that this is not Hog Hill – visited next!

To the east, **Tarras Moss** is where the dreaded Armstrong cattle-reivers retired to when pursuit was getting warm. In their time the place was tree covered between the boggy bits. It has been transformed and tamed by sheep and hillslope drainage.

At **Hog Fell** trig point turn half left to descend north-west over tussocky grass. As the slope curves over, the grassy ridge below running towards Hog Hill becomes visible. A stone sheepfold is at the start of this ridge. After 800 metres come to a sharp col. Either drop left to reach a track on the hill flank or keep ahead up **Hog Hill**, a viewpoint up and down Ewes valley, before descending south to join the same rough track.

The track runs down to **Hoghill farm** (pronounced 'hoggle') and passes to the left of the buildings to meet the A7 road opposite Sunny Brae cottage.

Cross to the left of Sunny Brae to a gate onto open hill above. Head straight up (passing a tiny crag) to the top of **Wrae Hill**.

Follow the grassy ridgeline down roughly south to a new grey metal gate in the wide col below – slightly down right of the actual col, Wrae Hass. The gate may have a waymark, 'Langholm Walks 4'. ▶

*Here turn down right for the more sheltered variant route (see below).*

Keep ahead to a gate with stile and waymark, and follow the remains of a former stone wall up the ridge south. On the way up Potholm Hill there's a trace of an ancient earthwork trench.

From **Potholm Hill** summit continue south, with the broken wall, to a wall corner with ladder stile. Cross and continue with a wall to your left over the southern top and then, with the wall turning away left, carry on to the end of the broad ridge at **Castle Hill**, overlooking Langholm.

Descend due south, through scattered thorns, and find a rough stony track starting. It leads to a gate and ladder stile at the hill foot. Take the track below, bearing left at a junction just below, to join the driveway below

*Heading down Castle Hill to Langholm*

225

a white house. Turn down this to a road triangle, where the ruined Langholm Castle is in a tree clump ahead. Turn left to cross the ancient Ewes Bridge to the Kiln Green **car park**.

**Return via Potholm farm**
From Wrae Hass, this route by the River Esk gives a more sheltered (if less interesting) finish.

At Wrae Hass col (south of **Wrae Hill**) turn down right, with the fence on the left, to a track above the valley floor. Turn left over a stile, and head down to a junction above **Potholm farm**. Here turn sharp left on a track rising gently through woods.

The track soon levels off and is followed through mixed woods (**Langfauld Wood**) for 1.7km. At a lodge house, keep right on the main track, passing above a fenced pheasant ranch to **Holmhead** farmyard. ◀

Turn down right in the farmyard, and in 50 metres bear right to a complex track junction. Keep straight across this and in 30 metres bear left on a small track. This narrows to become a riverside path along the River Esk.

After 1km ignore a white footbridge on your right. Keep on along the well-surfaced riverside path for another 500 metres to the end of a second footbridge, a black one. Again don't cross. From the path end, bear left away from the river to the ruin of Langholm Castle. Turn left behind the castle across grass to a gate near a lodge house. Turn right across Ewes Water to the **car park**.

*The track ahead becomes tarmac and leads straight to Langholm.*

# WALK 40
## *Cauldcleuch Head*

| | |
|---|---|
| **Start/Finish** | Twislehope track end (NY 452 967) |
| **Distance** | 22km (13½ miles) |
| **Ascent** | 900m (2900ft) |
| **Approx time** | 7½hrs |
| **Terrain** | Grassy ridges, track, quiet road |
| **Max altitude** | Cauldcleuch Head, 619m |
| **Maps** | Landranger 79 (Hawick); Explorers 324 (Liddesdale) and 331 (Teviotdale S) |
| **Parking** | Roadside at start or 400 metres east |
| **Variant** | Omitting Greatmoor Hill saves 4km (2½ miles) with 150m (500ft) of ascent (about 1¼hrs) |

Mary Queen of Scots was the saddest monarch Scotland has had, and one of the least effective. She was, however, a talented hill traveller. In 1566 she rode from Jedburgh to Hermitage Castle, by the hill paths, to visit her wounded lover the Earl of Bothwell. Then rode back again the same day – a total of about 45 miles.

Mary's pony-trek to the bed of the sexy scoundrel Bothwell made her even more unpopular than she already was with her Scots subjects, then engaged in converting themselves to Calvinism. The weather was so bad on the return journey that Mary fell dangerously ill. Later, during her long captivity in England, she said, 'Would that I had died at Jedburgh.'

After Mary's forced abdication, Bothwell fled to Denmark, where he was unlucky enough to be captured by a former lover, Anna Rustung. He spent the last ten years of his life chained to a wall in a dungeon. Yes, the history is miserable. The hill walk, however, with grassy paths to Cauldcleuch Head, the highest point hereabouts, is surprisingly enjoyable.

Follow the track across the cattle grid and the stream, then at once turn right along the stream side. After 200 metres pass through a gate in a field wall. Turn uphill to the right of the wall, and at its top pass through a gate onto Geordie's Hill. Go straight up through a gateway in a crossing fence, and follow remnants of a former wall ahead to **Geordie's Hill** summit.

*This point could have been reached by just walking up the road, but that route misses the great views down Hermitage and saves a mere 120m of ascent.*

Follow the fence down northwards. It reaches the road east of its highest point, opposite a plantation corner, and at the boundary between the Dumfries and Galloway Region and the Borders. ◄

Across the road keep ahead through a gateway onto a grassy quad-bike track, which leads up the spur of **Tudhope Hill**. Where the track fades, keep uphill near a fence to the trig point.

Follow the fence northeast, with a quad-bike path alongside. At **Millstone Edge** follow a side-fence to the right, south of east to start with and then northeast. It bends to the right around the head of **Langtae Sike** to the fence junction at the top of **Cauldcleuch Head**.

*On Tudhope Hill, heading towards Cauldcleuch Head*

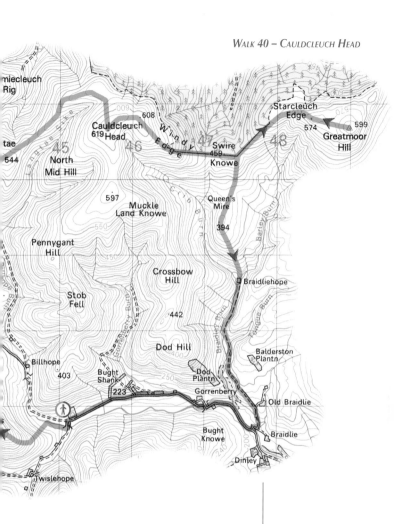

This point is a Graham, a Marilyn, and the County Top of Roxburghshire. More than that, it comprises an entire section (11 Roxburgh Hills) of **Donald's Tables**. Even so it boasts no cairn, as it's hard to build cairns out of cotton grass. Instead there's a tiny peat pool.

Alternatively, omit Greatmoor Hill and continue from here on the main route (see below).

Follow the side-fence to the left, northeast at first, bending southeast down **Windy Edge**, soon with trees to your left. Stay next to the plantation over the slight rise of **Swire Knowe** and then head up the long slope towards Greatmoor Hill. ◄

At the plantation's corner keep following the fence up the ridgeline of **Starcleuch Edge**. Above, there's a peaty levelling; a shepherd's path forking right and slightly downhill diverts around the small peat-hag zone here. Both routes – following the fence or the shepherd's path – rise to **Greatmoor Hill** summit, which has a trig point, a large cairn and views.

Return down Starcleuch Edge. At the forest corner before Swire Knowe, a path emerges through a small gate from the trees on your right. This ancient path was used by reivers and Queen Mary. Today it's just a groove in the grass as it is followed down to the left, south, around the flank of Swire Knowe. It drops into the wide col of **Queen's Mire**.

> The **Queen's Mire** is where Queen Mary almost came to grief on her ride to Hermitage Castle. According to Sir Walter Scott, the place in his time still showed the bones of horses drowned in the swampy bog. More recent field drains have spoiled the historical ambiance here.

Having survived the Queen's Mire, cross the knoll Winterlair Hill at 394m, then drop southeast through a gate in an electric fence and down to **Braidliehope** ruin in its hollow.

A well-made track continues down **Braidley Burn**. The track rises slightly across the hill flank above the stream, with views up the Hermitage Water, then drops to the valley road. Turn right for 1.5km along the quiet road to pass **Old Gorrenberry**.

> Hermitage valley is a haunt of the **bogle** Shellycoat, who lives in rivers and cries from underwater to bemuse lost travellers. In the dark you'll hear the

## HERMITAGE CASTLE

Hermitage is the grimmest of all the Border fortresses. It was built to dominate Liddesdale, the most dangerous part of all the lawless Border. In the 1560s its governor was Queen Mary's lover James Hepburn, Earl of Bothwell.

Bothwell was a soldier and adventurer and one of the murderers of the Queen Mary's husband Lord Darnley; even so he was only the third wickedest of the castle's various proprietors. And he took on more than he could manage when he tried singlehandedly to capture one of the local Border warlords, John Elliot of the Park. Hence his wound – and Mary's romantic ride.

The castle was restored to its original fierceness in the 19th century. The intimidating 'doorway' arches actually carried the fighting platform, a wooden balcony along the wall tops. As additional defence, imagine the castle surrounded by swamp.

There's a car park on the roadside and a footbridge, and a small entry charge. Outside opening hours you can wander the castle's exterior.

clattering of his shelly jacket. The bogle is mentioned by Sir Walter Scott, as is the brownie (Harry Potter fans – house elf) of Old Gorrenberry. There's a not very good picture of him on the front gate.

Another 1.5km along the road leads back to the walk start. Hermitage Castle is a few miles down the glen.

# WALK 41

*Peel Fell and Kielder Stone*

| | |
|---|---|
| **Start/Finish** | Roundabout at Kielder Castle (NY 631 934) |
| **Distance** | 25.5km (16 miles) |
| **Ascent** | 800m (2700ft) |
| **Approx time** | 9hrs |
| **Terrain** | Peaty bog and deep heather; woodland paths at start and end |
| **Max altitude** | Peel Fell, 602m |
| **Maps** | Landranger 80 (Cheviot Hills); Explorers OL42 (Kielder) and OL16 (Cheviot Hills) |
| **Parking** | Pay-and-display at Kielder Castle |

A hill walk ought to be enjoyable. This one is grim. From Deadwater Fell to Kielder Head the going is very rough, and in recent years what paths there are have been fading into the heather.

But it would be quite wrong for the Kielder Stone to be reached easily. This strange and atmospheric gritstone lump rising out of the heather was a border meeting place in the reiving times – when life itself was grim and unpleasant. Here among the mists and midges, march wardens and local warlords would get together on days of truce to see if there were any disputes that could be sorted out without the use of spears. It's also said that cross-border couples would leave love notes in the cracks of the rock. Today there's just a geocache message in a margarine tub.

*The red footprint waymarks guide to the top of Deadwater Fell.*

Take the roundabout exit opposite **Kielder Castle**, signed for Ravenshill Forest Lodges. The track is marked with a red footprint waymarker, 'Deadwater Walk'. Do not confuse this with plain red arrows that mark the difficult grade of mountain-bike trail. ◄

After 700 metres and before reaching the forest lodges, a path on the right is marked with a red footprint. The well-made path, with steps and handrails, rises above the track, then doubles back east to join a forest road.

Turn up left on a track rising northwest. At once ignore a red-arrow mountain-bike path forking left.

After rising through trees, the track drops a little. As trees restart, turn right up an old grassy track. At the top of the plantation, turn left on a good path. It crosses the Lightpipe Sike stream and rises to a forest road.

map continues on page 235

Turn uphill. Straight up now is another mountain-bike path, but the red footprint markers indicate the forest road that slants gently round to the left (west, then northwest) to a junction. Here turn right to slant up the other way to the top of the plantation.

Now the old track up to the left is the direct way to Deadwater Fell, and can be used if you're prepared to step aside when cyclists descend at breakneck pace with gravel flying from their fat wheels. The new, smooth track runs ahead over a cattle grid, then just below and east of Deadwater summit, before spiralling around left. Just after a cattle grid, turn up left, with a fence to your left, to the summit area and the trig point on **Deadwater Fell**.

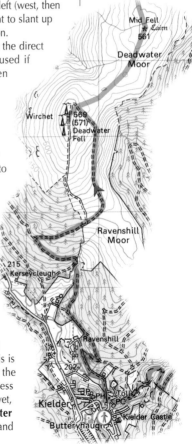

Deadwater Fell has radar and radio installations, an architect-designed bike shed, a claim of sea views on both sides of England and (somewhere hidden among the industrial superstructure) a trig point.

Follow the track northwards, and at the end of the buildings fork down right, with the fence to your right. (This is the path you arrived on if you chose the gentler ascent track.) Cross the access track just above the cattle grid onto a wet, peaty path northeast across **Deadwater Moor**. There are old iron fence posts, and

*Gritstone outcrop on Mid Fell, on the way to Peel Fell*

waymarks for the Kielderstane Trail unhelpfully spaced every kilometre or so.

The path passes to the right of a small pool, then gets drier as it rises to the cairn at Reivers Cross, summit of **Mid Fell**. ◀ The rough path continues bearing left (north-west) towards Peel Fell.

Two arms of the cross have rusted off, so it's now the Reivers L.

Just before the cairn, the path reaches a corner of old fence-post lines. Here a sign indicates the Kielderstane

*The Scottish Cairn, Peel Fell*

234

Trail turning right, but first follow the fence posts and path ahead to the English Cairn on **Peel Fell**.

> **Peel Fell** is where the border crosses the main watershed between the North Sea and the Solway Firth, and has been the start point for various Watershed walks to John o' Groats or Cape Wrath.

Continue along the old posts past a peat pool to the escarpment edge. Here are small gritstone edges, and 50 metres to the right is the Scottish Cairn – 3m lower than the English one, but with some rocks and much better views.

Return to the fence corner and Kielderstane signboard, and follow the fence posts northeast. A rough path follows the posts down a deeply heathery spur, then crosses a stream on the left to descend the parallel spur to the **Kielder Stone**.

map continues on page 237

> The ground around the **Kielder Stone** is grass rather than deep heather – some of it is dry, and there are sheltered nooks. Midges permitting, it's a fine place to spend the night. The Stone, which is jolly big, is most easily climbed at its northern corner, a steep and difficult scramble.
>
> The exact border line was important to the march wardens, who attempted to impose order here. Once day of border truce started with a handshake midstream in the Tweed! Acknowledging that this was an international meeting place, the England–Scotland border descends from the

235

*Down to the
Kielder Stone*

watershed here to pass through the centre of the
Stone – it returns to the ridgeline 1km to the north.
This makes Kielder Stone summit the least acces-
sible point on the borderline.

A small path contours north through the deep
heather, with border stones marked N (Northumberland)
and D (Douglas) – both letters upside down. Soon there
are old wooden posts as well. The path and posts dip to
cross a stream, climb steeply, and cross the moorland
flank of **Haggie Knowe** northeast. Then they descend a
spur to a stream junction.

Follow the right-hand stream, **Black Needle**, upstream
on grassy banks with frequent stream crossings. After 400
metres cross a small side-stream on the right, and then
as the stream bends to north–south head up the grassiest
streak you can pick northeast. Deep heather gets more
moderate as the slope eases, and heathery grass leads up
to the well-built summit cairn of **Knox Knowe**.

Head north, with boundary stones, fence posts and a very faint path across grassy peat moor. At the plateau edge it turns slightly right to descend to a wide, flat col. After 300 metres, turn down right on the map's bridleway line. The bridleway is unclear down out of the wide col, but a small path forms below and runs down to a ruin just above the **Carry Burn**.

The old path is visible as a grassy streak, which crosses a second stream immediately above a tiny waterfall. Next the fading path slants uphill along the top of steeper slopes, passing boulders and rock slabs, to a tall cairn above **Upper Stony Holes**.

Continue along the slope top for 200 metres, when the old path drops down the flank of **Grey Mares Knowe**. The path is visible mainly as a faint shelf in the heather, south. Around the very heathery hill slope it leads to a wide gap in trees. The tree gap is also very rough going, although it gets less bad as height is lost and grass replaces heather.

The gap passes through a clearing with bracken, then goes down to a ride crossing. But keep ahead down the untracked ride, and at its end follow a deer fence slightly to the right to exit from trees. Head down a field to the nearest building, **Kielder Head**. ▶

There's no right of way through Scaup farm ahead, so just above Kielder Head cross the stream and follow its left bank through a small gate. Once past the farm

map continues on page 238

This was once an open bothy, but returned to farm use in 2012.

opposite, head up the bank on your left, still following the river but now above the steep bank slope, and pass through a field gate with an old kissing gate.

Opposite where a track descends to the riverside on the other side, bear left slightly away from the river to find a bridleway gate. Cross the next field to **East Kielder farm**. Pass down to the right of the farm buildings to its access track, and follow this downhill to a bridge over **Kielder Burn**. ◄

Kielder Burn car park is just across this bridge.

Before the bridge, turn left on a forest road with a blue-arrow cycle-route waymark. Follow the gravel road for 3km until a wide path heads straight downhill to the right (another smaller path uphill is opposite.) The path descends to join a smooth-surfaced forest trail. Follow this to the right to a viewpoint above Kielder Burn, then go

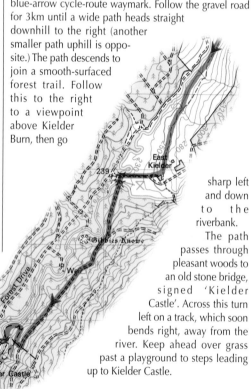

sharp left and down to the riverbank.

The path passes through pleasant woods to an old stone bridge, signed 'Kielder Castle'. Across this turn left on a track, which soon bends right, away from the river. Keep ahead over grass past a playground to steps leading up to Kielder Castle.

# WALK 42

*Hownam Law*

| | |
|---|---|
| **Start/Finish** | Morebattle (NT 772 248) |
| **Distance** | 16km (10 miles) |
| **Ascent** | 650m (2200ft) |
| **Approx time** | 5hrs |
| **Terrain** | Paths, grassy hillsides, field edges and tracks |
| **Max altitude** | Hownam Law, 449m |
| **Maps** | Landranger 74 (Kelso); Explorer OL16 (Cheviot Hills); Harveys Cheviot Hills |
| **Parking** | Street parking in Morebattle |

Nobody truly knows why the tribesmen of sometime Scotland and ancient England built earthworks around the tops of small pointy hills, then built huts inside the earthworks. Maybe the earthworks were, as the map calls them, forts for refuge against other nearby tribes. Maybe they lived high because the crops wouldn't grow down in the damp valleys.

Whatever it was they wanted, they found it in the Cheviots. Not on the wide bogs of the main ridge, but in the foothills on the Scottish side. Here any two valleys are separated by three or four small pointy hills, and every small pointy hill has its hill fort. One of the most shapely of them is Hownam Law, steep sided above the valleys of Kale Water and Bowmont. Whether for spotting intruding Romans, or simply looking up at the Cheviot ridge and out over the plains of the Tweed, Hownam's sight lines are outstanding.

This route uses Scotland's access privileges to pass through farmland. Use the route description to avoid climbing any walls or fences, and avoid disturbing farming activities. During lambing time (April and May) it would be better not to take a dog on this route, even on a short lead.

▸ At the east end of **Morebattle**, where the road bends left, keep ahead up a lane signed 'Hownam'. It soon drops to the **Kale Water**. Turn right, upvalley, again signed for Hownam, for 500 metres to a footbridge on the left.

For the first 4km to Wideopen Hill the route follows the waymarked St Cuthbert's Way.

Cross a field to join a track, and turn right on this. It passes up to the right of an old quarry, then zigzags uphill (vaguely east, then northeast) to a col. Turn right over a ladder stile to head uphill to the right of a plantation to a gate. The path continues straight uphill, through grass, to pass just to the left of the first hump summit, **Grubbit Law**.

Past the next col, the path rises to join a wall. It follows the main ridgeline, with the wall on its left, to a ladder stile on the second summit hump.

The path and wall continue to the third summit, **Wideopen Hill**, which a sign marks as the highest point of St Cuthbert's Way.

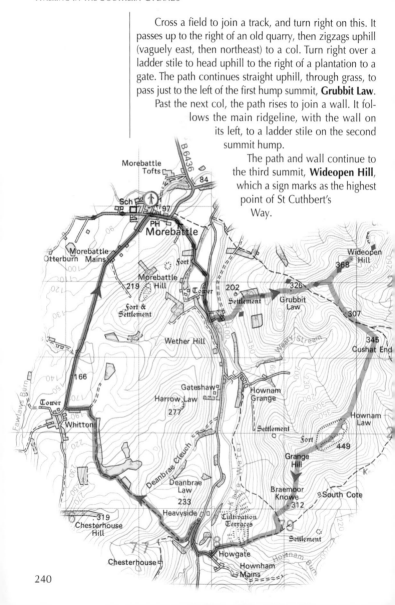

In its 100km (60 miles), the low-hill **St Cuthbert's Way** crosses the 1000ft (600m) contour four times – over the Eildon Hills; here; at the English border (Walk 44); and along moors between Hethpool and Wooler. It's a gentle and varied route that also includes the Tweed riverside and an optional mud crossing to Lindisfarne.

*St Cuthbert's Way path up Wideopen Hill*

Return southwest for 400 metres to the previous hump and turn down south, joining a wall on your right (the one crossed by the ladder stile). In the col this becomes a fence. It leads up, then bends to the right along **Cushat End**.

Below the final rise to Hownam Law, a field gate provides access through to the right-hand (west) side of the fence. Head up and to the right to where two walls form a corner. Here a gate gives access onto the heathery rough summit. Small paths lead up to the trig point on **Hownam Law**.

A little path leads along the short ridgeline southwest. Go down the steep end of the hill, avoiding a small crag, to pass a wall corner. Keep ahead to the left of the

*Down from Hownam Law towards Howgate*

wall for 100 metres, then go through a gate in it. Continue along the wall, following it around a bend to the left and downhill. Slant away from the wall, past a fence corner, onto the small hill **Braemoor Knowe**.

Descend southwest to a gate at the corner of two fences. Bear left and follow the fence south to a gate; go through and continue, now to the left of the fence. Go through a gate in a wall ahead and continue to another wall gate on the right. This gate is on the old path line marked on maps.

Turn downhill through the gate, descending with the fence to your right. At the field foot, a gate on the right leads to the top of a farm track. Go down this to **Howgate**, bearing left past the buildings to a tarmac drive. Turn right to the Kale Water road.

Turn right for 500 metres, crossing a bridge and rising gently to take a track turning sharply back to the left. After 400 metres this bends up to the right, northwest. It zig-zags left and right and then, high on the hill, goes through a gate. Here the track bends slightly to the right, but keep ahead alongside a wall to a small quarry before a wood.

Go through two gates to head along the left-hand side of the wood. Keep ahead to a larger plantation, and turn left alongside it. Follow the plantation edge round to the right and downhill.

At the plantation foot, a gate leads onto a grassy track. Turn left just below, passing the row of neat stone houses at **Whitton** to a road. Turn right, descending gently with wide views ahead into Morebattle.

## WALK 43
*Windy Gyle*

| | |
|---|---|
| **Start/Finish** | Mowhaugh, Bowmont Water (NT 814 208) |
| **Distance** | 26km (16 miles) |
| **Ascent** | 800m (2700ft) |
| **Approx time** | 8hrs |
| **Terrain** | Paths (sometimes very faint) and tracks |
| **Max altitude** | Windy Gyle, 619m |
| **Maps** | Landrangers 74 (Kelso) and 80 (Cheviot Hills); Explorer OL16 (Cheviot Hills); Harveys Cheviot Hills |
| **Parking** | Wide grass verges just south of the walk start, opposite Mowhaugh farm |
| **Variant** | Shorter route via The Street – 21km (13½ miles) with 550m (1750ft) of ascent (about 6½hrs) |

The main route by Cuthberthope Rig offers a long stretch of the border ridge, passing mysterious earthworks that once marked the border. The Pennine Way runs all along that border ridgeline, with sections of heathery bog all paved over with neat stone slabs. So the walking, wild and high, can also be easier than expected.

For an option that's not quite so long, the drove road of The Street, no longer knee deep in trampled cowpats, offers a smooth green highway to the heights. While there's only a couple of kilometres of the border ridgeline, those 2km are good ones.

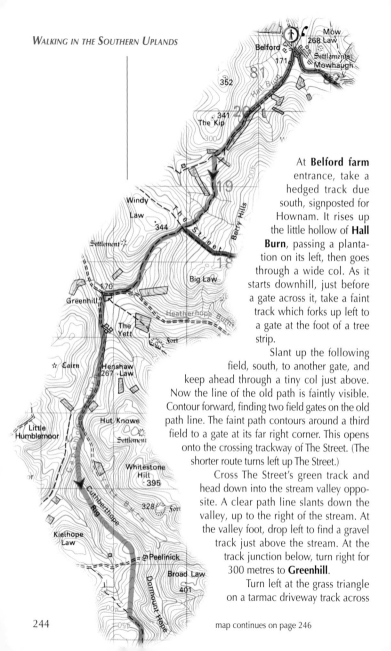

At **Belford farm** entrance, take a hedged track due south, signposted for Hownam. It rises up the little hollow of **Hall Burn**, passing a plantation on its left, then goes through a wide col. As it starts downhill, just before a gate across it, take a faint track which forks up left to a gate at the foot of a tree strip.

Slant up the following field, south, to another gate, and keep ahead through a tiny col just above. Now the line of the old path is faintly visible. Contour forward, finding two field gates on the old path line. The faint path contours around a third field to a gate at its far right corner. This opens onto the crossing trackway of The Street. (The shorter route turns left up The Street.)

Cross The Street's green track and head down into the stream valley opposite. A clear path line slants down the valley, up to the right of the stream. At the valley foot, drop left to find a gravel track just above the stream. At the track junction below, turn right for 300 metres to **Greenhill**.

Turn left at the grass triangle on a tarmac driveway track across

244                              map continues on page 246

Capehope Burn and up its valley. As the driveway bends left to recross the burn to **The Yett** farm, take a gate ahead onto a track that fords the burn just upstream from the farm's bridge.

Follow the track upvalley for 1.5km. As it bends left up the valley of Yett Burn, fork down right to a gate in a wall to the base of **Cuthberthope Rig**. Go straight up the grassy ridge, and follow it southeast over several humps.

In a final col cross a green track – it leads over to the abandoned shepherd's house **Peelinick**, out of sight down on the left. Head up through a gate in the fence just above, and follow the rising ridge south towards Raeshaw Fell. A raised grassy earthwork forms the path line – it runs along the gently rising ridge and up the steeper slope above. ▶

*To bag Raeshaw Fell, just keep straight on up the slope.*

Halfway up **Raeshaw Fell**, the path line slants left and takes a fine line along the brink of steep slopes dropping to Yett Burn.

The old path follows the line of the even older **Border Ditch**, although this is seen more clearly looking ahead, on the slope just north of the Lamb Hill Hut, and on the Scottish side of the border fence on the flank of Lamb Hill itself.

*Lamb Hill refuge hut, high on the Border Ridge*

The pathline, quite indistinct, continues east along the valley rim – if the path is lost, cross the fence 50 metres above on the right to find the Pennine Way path just beyond it. The older pathway eventually reaches a gate in that fence; don't go through, but follow the fence ahead for 100 metres to cross it by a stile next to the Lamb Hill Hut.

From here to Windy Gyle the route follows the Pennine Way, well trodden and occasionally waymarked, with the border fence alongside on its left. Up **Lamb Hill** the going is grassy, but this changes to peat and heather across the summit, with Lamb Hill's trig passed on the other side of the fence. The path is reinforced with stone slabs here and down to the following col.

After the next short rise, the path is again stone slabs as it bends right and crosses first **Beefstand Hill** and then **Mozie Law**, which has a tall waymark post marking its top. On the following descent the path bends right, short-cutting across the peat to rejoin the fence at another corner. Now slab free, it descends to a stile, gate and signpost as it meets **The Street**.

As indicated by the signpost, cross The Street's rough track half left on a path that rises gently across the moor, then dips to an abrupt little col. Above this the path rejoins the border fence at a 'Star of David' marker for an invisible archeological site. ◄

The shorter variant by The Street reaches the Border Ridge here.

map continues on page 249

## CROSSING THE CHEVIOTS

Today, the 40 miles (65km) of Border Ridge between Peel Fell (Walk 41) and Hethpool (Walk 44) is crossed by just one road, the A68 at Carter Bar. It used to be busier. The Romans' Dere Street, from York to the Scottish Lowlands, crossed at Chew Green (the fort there was known as Ad Fines, literally 'To the End of Everything'). Its next stop north was at Trimontium under the Eildons (Walk 31).

The green ridges and old roads made long-distance walking routes for the saints of the Dark Ages; St Cuthbert came this way between Iona and Lindisfarne.

In the lawless 16th century, the passes of the Cheviots became highways for the cattle thieves. And 200 years after that, those reivers' roads became the infrastructure of the cattle trade. The Street from Hownam to Coquetdale was an official drove road, and is still counted by the authorities today as a 'road', with a standard road sign 'No motors' at 500m high on the Border Ridge.

The grassy spur of **Windy Rig** (561m) ahead has two paths. The right-hand one, passing 50 metres down to the right of the ridgeline fence, has good situations

*Looking into Scotland from Windy Gyle*

overlooking Coquetdale and England. The paths rejoin along the narrow col beyond to rise alongside the border fence. A short way up the slope, take a waymarked gate through the fence and go up to the left of it. At the slope top, bear slightly left away from the fence to the trig point planted on the huge and ancient cairn of **Windy Gyle**.

> The cairn is considered to be a Bronze Age one. The name **Russell's Cairn** commemorates Lord Francis Russell, killed here on a day of border truce in 1585 – although historians think the other ancient cairn, 1km northeast, is where he was actually killed. The fact that a cairn commemorates his death does suggest that on these days of border truce the peace agreement did generally hold good.

Return back down the border fence – as you do so, the Windy Rig path north into Scotland is seen ahead. This time don't go through the waymarked gate, but stay to the right of the fence along the long col. At a fence junction just above, bear right, contouring round on a good wide path onto the northward Windy Rig. As the path bends right towards a very slight rise (520m), contour forward beside a fence to a gate at its corner.

Through this, go down to the right of a fence, which becomes a wall across a wide moorland col. At the low point, take a gate through the wall. Head out into the very rough moor (west), away from the wall, for about 150 metres to find (with great relief) a green tractor track.

Turn left along this track. In 100 metres it reaches the top of a wide, smooth gravel track. Follow this down into the valley of **Calroust Burn**. It heads downvalley, up to the left of the stream, passing **Calroust Hopehead** and in another 2km reaching the main farm, **Calroust**.

Wiggle left and right through the farmyard. The main driveway, a wide dirt track, bends right to cross the stream, but keep ahead through a gate to find a narrow, old tarmac driveway rising gently up the left side of the valley. This runs north through a couple of gates, becoming an unsurfaced track as it drops gently to the Bowmont Water road.

Turn left along the road to the walk start.

### Shorter route via the Street

The Street is an ancient drove road, now a wide green path with easy going. It makes a fine ascent route, but leaves you with a scant 2km of the actual Border Ridge to enjoy before turning back at Windy Gyle.

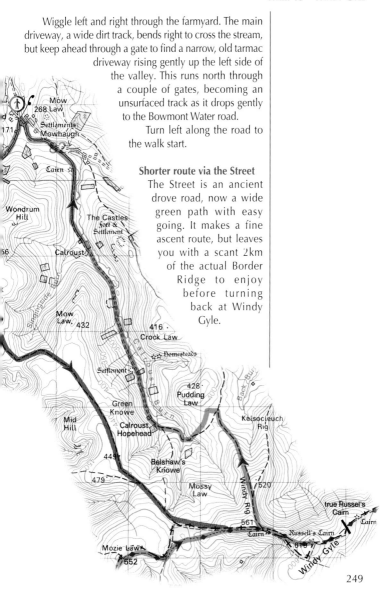

*Up the Street towards the Border Ridge*

Turn uphill on the green track of **the Street**, with a fence to its left. After a steep climb (the main climb – there is now only another 100m of height gain to the Border Ridge ahead) the track crosses the head of a stream valley running down to the right. The track dips to a col, where the main drovers' track continues on the left flank through two gates, outflanking a steepish rise ahead.

After regaining the wide ridge crest, the track dips slightly across pasture land, where it's not very clear across short-cropped grass. Keep ahead through a gate at the far right corner. The track continues with a fence to its right, going uphill slightly on the left flank of the wide ridgeline **Mid Hill**.

The track runs ahead past a signpost to a fence corner with a roadsign facing uphill ('No cars or motorbikes in April and May'). The gate ahead leads into England – but fork left on a fainter green track.

This track stays to the left of the border fence. It passes just down left of a col, curves left then back right, and arrives at a gate in the border fence. Through this, turn left, and continue back on the main route.

# WALK 44

*The Cheviot and Hen Hole*

| | |
|---|---|
| **Start/Finish** | Hethpool – estate car park 400 metres south of the hamlet (NT 893 280) |
| **Distance** | 29km (18 miles) |
| **Ascent** | 1000m (3300ft) |
| **Approx time** | 9½hrs |
| **Terrain** | Paths, peat bog, steep grass descent and rocky stream banks; 6km tarmac track to finish |
| **Max altitude** | The Cheviot, 815m |
| **Maps** | Landrangers 74 (Kelso) and 80 (Cheviot Hills); Explorer OL16 (Cheviot Hills); Harveys Cheviot Hills |
| **Parking** | Estate car park 400 metres south of Hethpool |

No hill of its height has a gentler ascent than the 12km of Border Ridge leading up to The Cheviot. It's pathed and waymarked, with one or two tiny tors to entertain, and the occasional boggy bits paved over with Pennine Way slabwork.

Everything changes at The Cheviot's swamp-surrounded trig point. There's a mile to walk through the peat pools and the heather, with some quite careful compass work (or the gps waypoint) to distract you from the black slime underfoot. After the navigation, the knees – on the steep drop into the Hen Hole. And then it's adventuring along the stream side, among the crags and waterfalls, in what has to be the Border Country's finest hill hollow.

Head north to **Hethpool**, turning left at the houses. ▶ Where the road bends right, take the tarred driveway track on the left, signed for Elsdon. It runs upvalley to the right of the stream. Ignore a side-track left, keeping ahead to **Elsdonburn**.

Zigzag back left (now on stony track) and back right through a gate above the house onto a grass pasture hill. The track runs southwest, bending left above the stream.

St Cuthbert waymarks now guide to the Border Ridge.

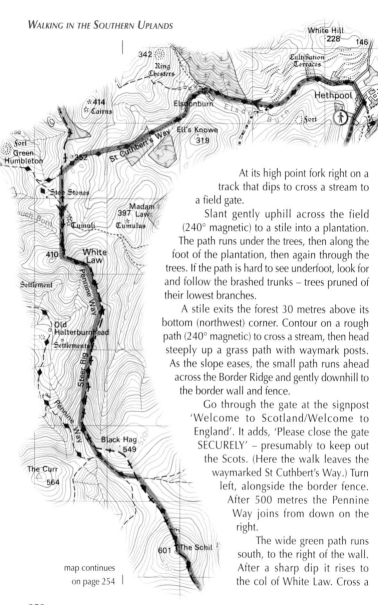

At its high point fork right on a track that dips to cross a stream to a field gate.

Slant gently uphill across the field (240° magnetic) to a stile into a plantation. The path runs under the trees, then along the foot of the plantation, then again through the trees. If the path is hard to see underfoot, look for and follow the brashed trunks – trees pruned of their lowest branches.

A stile exits the forest 30 metres above its bottom (northwest) corner. Contour on a rough path (240° magnetic) to cross a stream, then head steeply up a grass path with waymark posts. As the slope eases, the small path runs ahead across the Border Ridge and gently downhill to the border wall and fence.

Go through the gate at the signpost 'Welcome to Scotland/Welcome to England'. It adds, 'Please close the gate SECURELY' – presumably to keep out the Scots. (Here the walk leaves the waymarked St Cuthbert's Way.) Turn left, alongside the border fence. After 500 metres the Pennine Way joins from down on the right.

The wide green path runs south, to the right of the wall. After a sharp dip it rises to the col of White Law. Cross a

map continues on page 254

*The Cheviot from
Windy Gyle*

ladder stile over a wall. Turn left, with the fence to the
left, to the summit of **White Law**.

Bend right, south, still with a fence to your left. A
short but steep dip leads to the longer ascent of **Steer
Rig**. Through the gate at the top, the fence bears left to
the summit Black Hag, but the path keeps ahead (140°
magnetic) past a waymark and gently downhill for 250
metres to a signpost.

Here join the wide path of the lower-level Pennine
Way, contouring in from back right. Keep ahead on
this (120° magnetic) towards The Schil; then bend left
(ignoring a fainter grass path ahead) to rejoin the ridgeline wall at a ladder stile just north of a col. Across the
stile turn right with the wall on your right, and continue
on heathery ground through the col.

The path runs up past a tor on its left, then passes the
summit of **The Schil**, with its summit tor beyond the fence
on the right.

The Schil is made of pale grey or pinkish **rhyolite
lava**. Much of it is riddled with small holes, from the
gases dissolved in the lava that bubbled out as it hit

253

the open air. Some also shows yellowish feldspar crystals the size of porridge oats. On the back of the southern outcrop (near a brass memorial plaque) it's possible to pick out flow folding, the shape of the lava as it came to rest.

The path heads on down to cross a heathery shoulder, where it's reinforced with stone slabs. It follows its fence over a couple of bumps, then shortcuts past the top of an incised stream down left. In another 300 metres it rejoins the ridge fence at **Auchope Hut**, with its great view into Hen Hole opposite. (Anyone looking southwards up the College valley wouldn't suspect the presence of the Hen Hole tucked around the corner. And so, just like the Devil's Beef Tub (Walk 18), it was used as a hidey-hole for stolen cows.)

Path and fence drop to a final col for the stiff climb to **Auchope Cairn** – actually two square cairns among scree. Here walkers arrive on flat peaty bogland. The path (being rebuilt in stone slabs in summer 2013) runs ahead across this to a gate and signpost (Pennine Way three ways).

Turn left, signed for The Cheviot, on stone slabs. On the ascent towards

map continues on page 256

Cairn Hill, a fence joins from the right and the slabs end. They restart across **Cairn Hill** summit. At the signpost, bear slightly left without crossing any fence. The big sprawling shelter cairn lies to the right of the fence.

The slab path dips slightly past a murky little pool, then rises gently to **the Cheviot** summit. The trig point is mounted on a column of breeze blocks. ▸

Here the route leaves the Pennine Way waymarking.

Your direction for Hen Hole is west. However, west from the summit is a peat swamp. So retrace your steps along the stone pavement until opposite a less people-eating sort of swamp. Head west, soon finding ground with more grass in it, and as the plateau starts to slope away, a view of the surroundings appears. At this point aim your steps towards the pointed low hill Rubers Law, seen away out in the Tweed lowlands. Soon the ground steepens further, and you find yourself gazing down into the **Hen Hole**.

Streams run down into the Hole at both corners. The slope between is steep, but not too steep to get down. ▸ In the floor of the Hole, join the main stream as it runs out between granite crags. Where it has waterfalls, descent is always possible to the right of the water. If the

The left-hand stream, under Auchope Cairn, has pretty waterfalls.

*Hen Hole of the Cheviot*

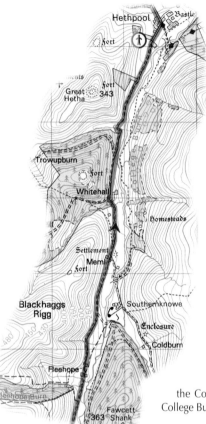

stream is in spate, passage may be awkward, as the easiest way crosses it quite often.

As the valley opens out below the Hole, keep to the left of the stream to find a grassy track. After a tin hut, this gradually becomes clearer. It passes through a broadleaf wood planted in 1995, then below a plantation to the bunkhouse at **Mounthooly**. Beyond Mounthooly the track is tarmac.

Halfway along the tarmac track is a memorial to 13 **World War Two aircraft** lost on The Cheviot. An aeroplane lost in cloud might risk a descent to 2500ft, in hope of seeing where it was. If very unlucky, it would hit the Cheviot – the only ground at that height in eastern Britain south of the Highlands.

The tarmac track runs down the College valley, always to the left of College Burn, to the car park at **Hethpool**.

# APPENDIX A
*Route summary table*

| No | Walk | Distance (km/miles) | Ascent (m/ft) | No of summits | Page |
|----|------|---------------------|---------------|---------------|------|
| **1 Galloway** | | | | | |
| 1 | Girvan and Grey Hill | 21 (13) | 750 (2500) | 2 | 25 |
| 2 | Ailsa Craig | 2.5 (1½) | 340 (1100) | 1 | 31 |
| 3 | Cairnsmore of Fleet | 14.5 (9) | 750 (2500) | 2 | 33 |
| 4 | Minnigaff Hills | 21 (13) | 1300 (4300) | 4 | 37 |
| 5 | Merrick and Murder Hole | 14.5 (9) | 700 (2700) | 2 | 42 |
| | variant: Rig of Buchan descent | 13.5 (8½) | 900 (3000) | | |
| 6 | The Dungeon Hills | 19 (12) | 1050 (3500) | 4 | 48 |
| | variant: the Three Lochs | 11.5 (7) | 600 (2000) | | |
| 7 | Rhinns of the Kells | 29 (18) | 1300 (4400) | 6 | 53 |
| | variant: southern Rhinns | 17.5 (11) | 950 (3100) | | |
| 8 | Cairnsmore of Carsphairn | 19 (12) | 1000 (3300) | 3 | 59 |
| 9 | Screel Hill | 8 (5) | 550 (1600) | 2 | 64 |
| | variant: omit Bengairn | 5 (3) | 350 (1100) | | |
| **2 Nithsdale and Lanarkshire** | | | | | |
| 10 | Afton Water | 13 (8) | 700 (2300) | 2 | 68 |
| 11 | Criffel | 12 (7½) | 600 (2000) | | 73 |
| | variant: shorter start | 9.5 (6) | 600 (2000) | | |
| 12 | Queensberry | 20 (12½) | 900 (3000) | 3 | 78 |
| | variant: from Earncraig Hill | 15 (9½) | 700 (2300) | | |
| 13 | Well Hill, Durisdeer | 9.5 (6) | 650 (2100) | 2 | 84 |
| 14 | Lowther Hill by Well and Enterkin passes | 24 (15) | 850 (2900) | 2 | 88 |
| | variant: include Well Hill | 26.5 (16½) | 1100 (3600) | | |
| | variant: via East Mount Lowther | 24 (15) | 950 (3100) | | |

| No | Walk | Distance (km/miles) | Ascent (m/ft) | No of summits | Page |
|---|---|---|---|---|---|
| 15 | Tinto | 11 (6¾) | 500 (1700) | 1 | 94 |
| 16 | Culter Fells | 18.5 (11½) | 700 (2300) | 2 | 98 |
| | variant: Chapelgill Hill | 20.5 (13) | 700 (2300) | | |
| 17 | Broughton Heights | 14.5 (9) | 1100 (3800) | 3 | 102 |
| **3 Moffatdale** | | | | | |
| 18 | Devil's Beef Tub | 10 (6) | 550 (1800) | 1 | 108 |
| 19 | Ettrick Head | 19 (11½) | 1000 (3300) | 4 | 113 |
| | variant: omit Loch Fell | 16 (10) | 850 (2800) | | |
| 20 | Hart Fell | 15 (9½) | 900 (3000) | 4 | 118 |
| | variant: Swatte Fell summit | 15.5 (9¾) | 900 (3000) | | |
| 21 | White Coomb | 12 (7½) | 750 (2500) | 2 | 123 |
| | variant: Dobb's Linn | 13 (8) | 850 (2800) | | |
| 22 | White Coomb and Hart Fell | 28 (17½) | 1200 (4000) | 6 | 129 |
| | variant: Swatte Fell summit | 28.5 (17¾) | 1200 (4000) | | |
| 23 | Loch of the Lowes and Ward Law | 15 (9) | 550 (1900) | 2 | 134 |
| | variant: Peniestone Knowe only | 10.5 (6½) | 400 (1300) | | |
| 24 | The Wiss and St Mary's Loch | 14.5 (9) | 400 (1200) | 1 | 139 |
| | variant: combine 23 and 24 | 24 (15) | 800 (2600) | 3 | |
| **4 Manor Hills to the Tweed** | | | | | |
| 25 | Broad Law | 21 (13) | 800 (2700) | 4 | 144 |
| 26 | Manor Head | 22 (14) | 1100 (3700) | 4 | 149 |
| 27 | Cademuir Hill and the Tweed | 12.5 (7½) | 300 (1000) | 1 | 153 |
| 28 | Glen Sax Circuit | 26 (16) | 1000 (3300) | 5 | 157 |
| | variant: River Tweed finish | 27.5 (17) | 950 (3200) | | |
| 29 | Lee Pen and Windlestraw Law | 27 (17) | 1050 (3500) | 3 | 164 |
| | variant: Lee Pen and Leithen | 13 (8) | 600 (1900) | | |

| No | Walk | Distance (km/miles) | Ascent (m/ft) | No of summits | Page |
|----|------|---------------------|---------------|---------------|------|
| 30 | Three Brethren and Minch Moor | 21 (13½) | 750 (2500) | 2 | 170 |
|    | variant: omit Minch Moor summit | 15 (9½) | 550 (1800) | | |
| 31 | Eildon Hills and the Tweed | 22.5 (14) | 750 (2500) | 3 | 175 |
|    | variant: omit Tweed | 15.5 (9½) | 650 (2200) | | |
| 32 | Rubers Law | 12 (7½) | 450 (1500) | 1 | 182 |
| **5 Lothian** | | | | | |
| 33 | Pentlands | 25 (15½) | 1100 (3700) | 7 | 189 |
|    | variant: back by Glencorse lane | 15.5 (9½) | 750 (2500) | | |
| 34 | Arthur's Seat | 4 (2½) | 300 (1000) | 1 | 194 |
| 35 | Blackhope Scar | 23.5 (14½) | 500 (1700) | 1 | 197 |
| 36 | Lammer Law | 14 (9) | 400 (1300) | 1 | 202 |
|    | variant: road via Longyester | 15.5 (10) | 400 (1300) | | |
| 37 | Abbey St Bathans and Cockburn Law | 12.5 (8) | 350 (1100) | 1 | 206 |
| 38 | North Berwick Law | 31 (19½) | 300 (1000) | 1 | 210 |
|    | variant: Gullane start | 24.5 (15½) | 250 (800) | | |
| **6 The Border Ridge to Cheviot** | | | | | |
| 39 | Langholm Heights | 15.5 (9½) | 700 (2300) | 4 | 221 |
| 40 | Cauldcleuch Head | 22 (13½) | 900 (2900) | 3 | 227 |
|    | variant: omit Greatmoor Hill | 18 (11) | 750 (2400) | | |
| 41 | Peel Fell and Kielder Stone | 25.5 (16) | 800 (2700) | 2 | 232 |
| 42 | Hownam Law | 16 (10) | 650 (2200) | 2 | 239 |
| 43 | Windy Gyle | 26 (16) | 800 (2700) | 2 | 243 |
|    | variant: The Street | 21 (13½) | 550 (1750) | | |
| 44 | The Cheviot and Hen Hole | 29 (18) | 1000 (3300) | 5 | 251 |

# APPENDIX B

*Information and facilities by area*

## 1 Galloway

### Tourist information

Ayr
01292 290300

Newton Stewart
01671 402431

Castle Douglas
01556 502611

Forestry Commission visitor centre
Stroan Bridge (NX 372 786)
closed Oct – Feb

Galloway Forest Park
www.gallowayforestpark.com

### Local transport

Stagecoach 500 Dumfries to Newton Stewart for Stranraer, seven times daily. Newton Stewart has good bus links with Dumfries (and a nightly international coach to Belfast or London). Infrequent local buses to Glentrool village and Forrest Lodge track end.

### Facilities

Walks 4–6: Bargrennan has camp site and good pub, with a visitor centre and tea room at Stroan Bridge (closed winter).

Walks 7–8: New Galloway/Dalry have shops, pubs and petrol station.

### Hostels and bothies

Culsharg bothy, on the main path up Merrick, has been recently renovated and is now midgeproof and dry; White Laggan and Tunskeen are also in the main Galloway Hills (Backhill of Bush and Shiel of Castlemaddie are defunct). Glennoch lies east of Cairnsmore of Carsphairn.

SYHA Minnigaff at Newton Stewart
01671 402211

Galloway Activity Centre, Loch Ken
01644 420626
www.lochken.co.uk

### Local guides

*Walking the Galloway Hills*
by Paddy Dillon (Galloway Hills main area north of A712)

*Walking the Lowther Hills*
by Ronald Turnbull (Cairnsmore of Fleet and rest of area)

## 2 Nithsdale and Lanarkshire

### Tourist information

Dumfries
01387 253862

Biggar
WP Bryden Newsagents
01899 220069

www.visitlanarkshire.com

## Local transport

The Glasgow–Dumfries railway allows walks from New Cumnock, Kirkconnel and Sanquhar, including station-to-station links.

The useful bus 101/102 Edinburgh–Dumfries passes through Dalveen Pass to Durisdeer Mill three times daily. Local buses link Thornhill to Dumfries, New Cumnock to Ayr and Dumfries, Broughton to Biggar. Infrequent local buses to Durisdeer.

## Facilities

Walks 13–14: Durisdeer has home-baked afternoon tea on summer Sundays in the room above the church.

Walk 10: New Cumnock is a depressed mining village – accommodation is basic and inexpensive.

Walk 17: Broughton has shop, café and pub.

## Hostels and bothies

SYHA New Lanark
01555 666710

Bunkhouse Marthrown of Mabie
01387 247900
www.marthrownofmabie.com

Kettleton Byre bothy above Durisdeer

Burleywhag below Queensberry

Brattleburn west of the M74

## Local guides

*Walking the Lowther Hills*
by Ronald Turnbull

*Walks in the Lammermuirs*
by Alan Hall (Culter Fells and Broughton Heights)

## 3 Moffatdale

### Tourist information

Moffat
01683 220134

### Local transport

Bus 101/102 Edinburgh–Dumfries via Moffat arrives by M74 (not Devil's Beef Tub). Coaches also from Carlisle and Glasgow.

### Facilities

St Mary's Loch has Glen Café and Tibbie Shiel's Inn.

### Hostels and bothies

Over Phawhope bothy on SU Way at Ettrick Head; Gamsehope bothy north of Hart Fell.

### Local guide

*The Border Country*
by Alan Hall

## 4 Manor Hills to the Tweed

### Tourist information

Melrose
01896 822283

Hawick
01450 373993

www.bordersabbeysway.com

www.stcuthbertsway.info

## Local transport

Good bus links from Edinburgh to Peebles, and from both Edinburgh and Berwick to Galashiels and Melrose. School bus to Yarrowford from Selkirk.

## Hostels and bothies

Broadmeadows Youth Hostel has closed. Minchmoor bothy above Traquair on SU Way.

## Local guides

*The Border Country*
by Alan Hall

www.southofscotlandcountrysidetrails.co.uk

## 5 Lothian

### Tourist information

Edinburgh
0845 225 5121

Pentland Hills Regional Park
www.pentlandhills.org

Flotterstone Visitor Centre
01968 677879

North Berwick
01620 92197

### Local transport

Bus 101/102 Edinburgh–Dumfries via either Thornhill or Moffat, six times daily along the base of the Pentland Hills. Haddington and North Berwick have good bus links to Edinburgh.

## Facilities

Walk 37: Abbey St Bathans has a restaurant, the Riverside.

## Hostels and bothies

Edinburgh has a wide range of hostels, including two SYHA.

## Local guides

*The Pentland Hills: A Walker's Guide*
by Susan Falconer

*Walks in the Lammermuirs*
by Alan Hall

## 6 The Border

### Tourist information

Gretna
01461 337834

www.langholm-online.co.uk

Hermitage Castle
www.historic-scotland.gov.uk

Kielder Forest Park
www.visitkielder.com

Northumberland National Park
www.northumberlandnationalpark.org.uk

Wooler
01668 282123

Kelso
01573 228055

www.stcuthbertsway.info

## Local transport

Langholm has hourly coaches from Carlisle and Edinburgh. Bus 128 Newcastleton–Hawick passes near Hermitage. Kielder bus 880 to Hexham twice daily, www.travelinenortheast.info. Kirk Yetholm has five daily buses to/from Kelso – Munros of Jedburgh bus 81, 01835 862253 – with bus links to Berwick and Edinburgh.

## Facilities

Walk 40: Newcastleton has pubs and a shop.

Walk 41: Kielder has shop, café, pub and community petrol station.

Walks 42–43: Morebattle has a shop and good pub, www.templehallhotel.com.

## Hostels and bothies

SYHA Kirk Yetholm
01573 420639

YHA Wooler
www.woolerhostel.co.uk

YHA affiliate Mounthooly Bunkhouse at head of College valley below Cheviot
01668 216358
www.college-valley.co.uk

Upper Eskdale has Dryfehead and Greensykes bothies.

Will's bothy is at Riccarton Junction, 4km northeast of Hermitage.

Spithope bothy is just south of the Border Ridge east of Carter Bar.

Simple wooden sheds are on the Cheviot ridge at Lamb Hill and Auchope Cairn.

## Local guides

*Walking the Lowther Hills*
by Ronald Turnbull (Langholm, Cauldcleuch Head)

*The Border Country*
by Alan Hall

# APPENDIX C
*Scots glossary*

The Southern Uplands is where three languages collide. Lallans – Lowland Scots – gives us the burns, cleuchs and linns, and names the hills as Laws. How do other hill-speakers manage without the useful term 'hope'? It means a closed-in upland hollow, a place for shielings where the herds can pass the summer. But the Norsemen also rampaged here, so valleys are dales, and the hills that aren't Laws are Fells. The Nordic 'hass', familiar in Lakeland as 'hause', means a pass in many Border placenames.

But before the Scots and the Norsemen, there were the Celts. Their Gallovidian language was related to the Gaelic of the north. Penbane (several of them) could be familiar as 'Beinn Bhan' (the white hill), while Kirriereoch is 'Coire Riabhach' (the speckled corrie). But altogether other are names like Mullwarchar and Merrick – the original Celtic misspelt and mispronounced by later generations to make the distinctive hill names of Galloway. And it probably took all three languages to twist out a name like the Rig of the Jarkness.

| Scots | English |
|---|---|
| *birk* | birch tree |
| *blackmail* | protection money or insurance premium paid to local warlord against cattle thieves ('mail' = rent) |
| *bogle* | a scary monster, the boggart or bogie-man (tattie-bogle = potato monster, ie a scarecrow) |
| *bughts* | sheep-handling pens |
| *burn* | stream |
| *cleuch* | deeply incut stream or gorge |
| *conventicle* | Covenanters' secret and usually open-air religious ceremony |
| *Covenanter* | extremist Presbyterian Protestant of the late 17th century, heavily persecuted by king and government |
| *dod* | a rounded, upstanding hill |
| *driech* | dull, dismal (weather or people) |
| *drive* | hill road suitable for driving in carriages, typically by duchesses |
| *drove road* | long-distance path used for driving cattle, especially on the autumn journeys to markets in the south |
| *flow* | bog |

| Scots | English |
|---|---|
| *gimmer* | female sheep two years old, up to having her first lamb |
| *hart* | deer (Norse) |
| *hass* | hill pass (Norse; 'hause' in Lake District) |
| *hogg* | female sheep between one and two years old |
| *hope* | high hollow between the hills – such places often used as summer pasture above the main farm |
| *knowe* | knoll |
| *law* | hill, especially an isolated one; also a grave mound |
| *linn* | stream between high rock walls |
| *martyr* | covenanter killed by the authorities |
| *merk* | coin valued at 6s 8d |
| *moss* | bog |
| *peewee, peewit* | lapwing |
| *pele, peel* | tower for refuge against cattle-raiding neighbours |
| *pen* | steep pointed hill (Gaelic 'Beinn') |
| *pennyland, merkland* | farm names reflecting original rental value |
| *reiver* | long-distance pony-trekking raider and cattle thief (hence 'bereaved') |
| *rig* | ridge |
| *road* | hill path suitable for horsemen, especially for reiving raids |
| *scar, scaur* | eroded hillslope of scree, stones and rock (hence Scawd Law, Scald Law) |
| *shaw* | small wood or thicket; a hill slope narrow at the top |
| *shiel* | shieling, summer pasture ground |
| *sike* | small stream |
| *stob* | fence post or any sort of spike |
| *tup* | ram (male sheep) |
| *watch* | lookout (Watch Hill, Watch Knowe, etc) |
| *wedder* | castrated male sheep |
| *whaup* | curlew |

*Merrick (Walk 5) and Loch Valley from Rig of the Jarkness*

# NOTES

# The Great Outdoors

**DIGITAL** EDITIONS

# 30-DAY FREE TRIAL

- Substantial savings on the newsstand price and print subscriptions
- Instant access wherever you are, even if you are offline
- Back issues at your fingertips

Downloading **The Great Outdoors** to your digital device is easy, just follow the steps below:

**1** **Download the App** from the App Store

**2** **Open the App**, click on 'subscriptions' and choose an annual subscription

**3** **Download** the latest issue and enjoy

Available on the **App Store**

The digital edition is also available on

The 30-day free trial is not available on Android or Pocketmags and is only available to new subscribers

 **pocketmags**.com

# LISTING OF CICERONE GUIDES

Walking in Corsica
Walking in Provence – East
Walking in Provence – West
Walking in the Auvergne
Walking in the Cevennes
Walking in the Dordogne
Walking in the Haute Savoie –
    North & South
Walking in the Languedoc
Walking in the Tarentaise and
    Beaufortain Alps
Walks in the Cathar Region

## GERMANY
Germany's Romantic Road
Hiking and Biking in the
    Black Forest
Walking in the Bavarian Alps

## HIMALAYA
Annapurna
Bhutan
Everest
Garhwal and Kumaon
Langtang with Gosainkund
    and Helambu
Manaslu
The Mount Kailash Trek
Trekking in Ladakh
Trekking in the Himalaya

## ICELAND & GREENLAND
Trekking in Greenland
Walking and Trekking in Iceland

## IRELAND
Irish Coastal Walks
The Irish Coast to Coast Walk
The Mountains of Ireland

## ITALY
Gran Paradiso
Sibillini National Park
Shorter Walks in the Dolomites
Through the Italian Alps
Trekking in the Apennines
Trekking in the Dolomites
Via Ferratas of the Italian
    Dolomites: Vols 1 & 2
Walking in Abruzzo
Walking in Italy's Stelvio
    National Park
Walking in Sardinia
Walking in Sicily
Walking in the Central
    Italian Alps

Walking in the Dolomites
Walking in Tuscany
Walking in Umbria
Walking on the Amalfi Coast
Walking the Italian Lakes

## MEDITERRANEAN
Jordan – Walks, Treks, Caves,
    Climbs and Canyons
The Ala Dag
The High Mountains of Crete
The Mountains of Greece
Treks and Climbs in Wadi Rum
Walking in Malta
Western Crete

## NORTH AMERICA
British Columbia
The Grand Canyon
The John Muir Trail
The Pacific Crest Trail

## SOUTH AMERICA
Aconcagua and the
    Southern Andes
Hiking and Biking Peru's
    Inca Trails
Torres del Paine

## SCANDINAVIA
Walking in Norway

## SLOVENIA, CROATIA AND
## MONTENEGRO
The Islands of Croatia
The Julian Alps of Slovenia
The Mountains of Montenegro
Trekking in Slovenia
Walking in Croatia
Walking in Slovenia: The
    Karavanke

## SPAIN AND PORTUGAL
Costa Blanca: West
Mountain Walking in
    Southern Catalunya
The Mountains of Central Spain
The Mountains of Nerja
The Northern Caminos
Trekking through Mallorca
Walking in Madeira
Walking in Mallorca
Walking in Menorca
Walking in the Algarve
Walking in the Cordillera
    Cantabrica

Walking in the Sierra Nevada
Walking on Gran Canaria
Walking on La Gomera and
    El Hierro
Walking on La Palma
Walking on Lanzarote and
    Fuerteventura
Walking on Tenerife
Walking the GR7 in Andalucia
Walks and Climbs in the
    Picos de Europa

## SWITZERLAND
Alpine Pass Route
Central Switzerland
The Bernese Alps
The Swiss Alps
Tour of the Jungfrau Region
Walking in the Valais
Walking in Ticino
Walks in the Engadine

## TECHNIQUES
Geocaching in the UK
Indoor Climbing
Lightweight Camping
Map and Compass
Mountain Weather
Moveable Feasts
Outdoor Photography
Polar Exploration
Rock Climbing
Sport Climbing
The Book of the Bivvy
The Hillwalker's Guide to
    Mountaineering
The Hillwalker's Manual

## MINI GUIDES
Alpine Flowers
Avalanche!
Navigating with a GPS
Navigation
Pocket First Aid and
    Wilderness Medicine
Snow

## MOUNTAIN LITERATURE
8000 metres
A Walk in the Clouds
Unjustifiable Risk?

For full information on all our
guides, books and eBooks,
visit our website:
**www.cicerone.co.uk**.

## Walking – Trekking – Mountaineering – Climbing – Cycling

**Over 40 years, Cicerone have built up an outstanding collection of 300 guides, inspiring all sorts of amazing adventures.**

Every guide comes from extensive exploration and research by our expert authors, all with a passion for their subjects. They are frequently praised, endorsed and used by clubs, instructors and outdoor organisations.

All our titles can now be bought as **e-books** and many as iPad and Kindle files and we will continue to make all our guides available for these and many other devices.

Our website shows any **new information** we've received since a book was published. Please do let us know if you find anything has changed, so that we can pass on the latest details. On our **website** you'll also find some great ideas and lots of information, including sample chapters, contents lists, reviews, articles and a photo gallery.

It's easy to keep in touch with what's going on at Cicerone, by getting our monthly **free e-newsletter**, which is full of offers, competitions, up-to-date information and topical articles. You can subscribe on our home page and also follow us on **Facebook** and **Twitter**, as well as our **blog**.

**Cicerone – the very best guides for exploring the world.**

# CICERONE

2 Police Square  Milnthorpe  Cumbria  LA7 7PY
Tel: 015395 62069  info@cicerone.co.uk
www.cicerone.co.uk